Union Pacific Railway Company

A Description of the western Resorts for Health and Pleasure

reached via Union Pacific Railway

Union Pacific Railway Company

A Description of the western Resorts for Health and Pleasure reached via Union Pacific Railway

ISBN/EAN: 9783337148164

Printed in Europe, USA, Canada, Australia, Japan

Cover: Foto ©Lupo / pixelio.de

More available books at **www.hansebooks.com**

UNION PACIFIC

THE OVERLAND ROUTE

A DESCRIPTION

of the

Western Resorts

for

Health AND Pleasure

reached via

UNION PACIFIC RAILWAY.

OVERLAND ROUTE.

Compliments of the
Passenger Department.

Rand McNally & Co.
Printers, Chicago

OFFICERS UNION PACIFIC RAILWAY.

CHARLES FRANCIS ADAMS, President,	Boston, Mass.
THOS. L. KIMBALL, Acting General Manager,	Omaha, Neb.
JOHN S. CAMERON, Assistant to Acting General Manager,	Omaha, Neb.

J. S. TEBBETS, General Passenger and Ticket Agent,	Omaha, Neb.
E. L. LOMAX, Assistant General Passenger and Ticket Agent,	Omaha, Neb.
J. A. MUNROE, General Freight Agent,	Omaha, Neb.
H. A. JOHNSON, First Assistant General Freight Agent,	Omaha, Neb.
F. B. WHITNEY, Assistant General Freight Agent,	Kansas City, Mo.
D. B. KEELER, Assistant General Freight Agent,	Denver, Colo.
W. H. BALDWIN, JR., Division Freight Agent,	Butte, Mont.
J. V. PARKER, Division Freight and Passenger Agent,	Salt Lake City, Utah.
D. W. HITCHCOCK, General Agent,	San Francisco, Cal.
J. A. S. REED, General Traveling Agent, Passenger Department,	Chicago, Ill.
R. TENBROECK, General Eastern Agent,	New York.
J. M. BECHTEL, General Agent,	Chicago, Ill.
J. F. AGLAR, General Agent,	St Louis, Mo.
J. D. WELCH, General Agent,	Cincinnati, O.
A. TRAYNOR, General Baggage Agent,	Council Bluffs, Ia.
E. DICKINSON, General Superintendent,	Omaha, Neb.
J. O. BRINKERHOFF, Superintendent Kansas Division,	Kansas City, Mo.
R. BLICKENSDERFER, Superintendent Nebraska Division.	Omaha, Neb.
J. K. CHOATE, Superintendent Colorado Division,	Denver, Colo.
C. E. WURTELE, Superintendent Wyoming Division,	Cheyenne, Wyo.
C. F. RESSEGUIE, Superintendent Idaho Division,	Pocatello, Idaho.
W. W. RITER, Superintendent Salt Lake and Western Division,	Salt Lake City, Utah.

INDEX.

HEALTH AND PLEASURE RESORTS.

My country, 'tis of thee,
Sweet land of liberty,
Of thee I sing :

*　*　*　*　*　*

I love thy rocks and rills,
Thy woods and templed hills ;
My heart with rapture thrills
Like that above.

THE question, "Where shall we go for health and pleasure?" assumes greater importance each succeeding year with the American public, and these pages have been written to assist those who are in doubt in settling this important point, as well as to show them what a wonderful country lies between the Missouri River and the Pacific coast.

Americans go to Europe to see Switzerland and the Rhine, to spend a winter in Italy, to do the Pyrenees and the Alps, to visit the German spas, the Highlands of Scotland, the Giant's Causeway of Ireland, and other places of interest ; when right in their own country, almost at their doors, are rivers, forests, lakes and mountains, and medicinal springs, rivaling the Pool of Bethesda of old ; sublime scenery bordering on the weird and supernatural, quiet vales and dells far excelling those of Europe, or any other portion of the civilized world. These places, too, are easy of access, and it is not necessary to learn a foreign language to be able to enjoy them.

Following up the sentiment so generally expressed nowadays, America for scenery, it is important that every American, native or naturalized, should post himself, as a matter of patriotism and pride, on the resources and characteristics of his own country.

Nowhere on the globe is there to be found such a variety of climate, scenery, and resources, as between the Missouri River, or the ninety-sixth meridian, and the Pacific Ocean ; and in this magnificent stretch of country are found resorts which can be enjoyed at all seasons of the year. The best climate of every known country can be found in this area. Here nature not only equals, but excels, everything that she has done for mankind in other portions of the globe; and American enterprise and skill have made them accessible to the nations of the earth.

To a vast majority of our people this great country was, until within the last few years, practically a sealed book, when its treasures of climate, scenery, and products were opened up to the world, by the original completion and the later extension of the Union Pacific Railway, "THE OVERLAND ROUTE."

It will be found that only a few of the most attractive and important points on this great transcontinental highway have been mentioned in the following pages, because suitable accommodations have not as yet been prepared at all of them for the tourist, and the health and pleasure seeker. There are hundreds of other points that only await the magic touch of progress to awake from the sleep of ages, as did the fabled princess who awaited the coming of her prince. Year by year, more and more of these resorts will be developed for the entertainment and benefit of mankind.

If these pages shall arouse the patriotism of Americans, and induce them to acquaint themselves with the great resources of their own country; with the wonderful cures nature provides at the health resorts for all the ills that flesh is heir to; with the facilities for enjoyment at the pleasure resorts that the Union Pacific Railway offers them along its lines in "The Far West," then their mission will have been accomplished.

GENERAL INFORMATION.

LIST OF AGENTS.

Baltimore, Md.—217 East Baltimore street.—D. E. BURLEY, Traveling Passenger Agent.

Boston Mass.—290 Washington street.—W. S. CONDELL, New England Freight and Passenger Agent.
    J. S. SMITH, Traveling Passenger Agent.
    E. M. NEWBEGIN, Traveling Freight and Passenger Agent.
    A. P. MASSEY, Passenger and Freight Solicitor.

Buffalo, N. Y.—40½ Exchange street.—S. A. HUTCHISON, Traveling Passenger Agent.

Butte, Mon. Ter.—Corner Main and Broadway.—W. H. BALDWIN, Jr., General Agent.

Chicago, Ill.—191 Clark street.—J. M. BECHTEL, General Agent Passenger and Freight Departments.
    T. W. YOUNG, Traveling Passenger Agent.
    W. T. HOLLY, City Passenger Agent.

Cincinnati, O.—169 Walnut street.—J. D. WELSH, General Agent Freight and Passenger Departments.
    H. C. SMITH, Traveling Freight and Passenger Agent.

Cleveland, O.—Kennard House.—A. G. SHEARMAN, Traveling Freight and Passenger Agent.

Columbus, O.—N. W. Corner Gay and High streets.—T. C. HIRST, Traveling Passenger Agent.

Council Bluffs, Ia.—U. P. Transfer.—W. H. BURNS, General Agent.
    M. J. GREEVY, Passenger Agent.
    J. W. MAYNARD, Ticket Agent.

Denver, Colo.—1,703 Larimer street.—D. B. KEELER, Assistant General Freight Agent and General Agent Passenger Department.
    H. J. RIFENBERICK, Traveling Passenger Agent.
    F. B. SEMPLE, City Passenger Agent.

Des Moines, Ia.—218 Fourth street.—E. M. FORD, Traveling Passenger Agent.

Detroit, Mich.—62 Griswold street.—D. W. JOHNSTON, Michigan Passenger Agent.

Helena, Mon. Ter.—24 Main street.—A. C. VEAZIE, Traveling Passenger Agent.

Indianapolis, Ind.—69 West Maryland street.—C. S. BLACKMAN, Traveling Passenger Agent.

Kansas City, Mo.—Ninth and Broadway.—F. B. WHITNEY, General Agent Passenger Department
    and Assistant General Freight Agent.
    J. B. REESE, Traveling Passenger Agent.
    E. W. McKEON, Union Depot, Passenger Agent.
    T. A. SHAW, Ticket Agent, 1,038 Union avenue.
    A. W. MILLSPAUGH, Ticket Agent, Union Depot.
    C. A. WHITTIER, City Ticket Agent, 528 Main street.

London, England.—THOS. COOK & SONS, European Agents, Ludgate Circus.
    C. A. GILLIG, Agent, United States Exchange, 9 Strand, Charing Cross.

Los Angeles, Cal.—236 North Main street.—A. J. HECHTMAN, Agent Passenger and Freight
    Departments.

Louisville, Ky.—346 West Main street.—N. HAIGHT, Traveling Passenger Agent.

Montreal, Can.—136 St. James street.—JAS. DUNN, Canadian Freight and Passenger Agent.

New York City.—287 Broadway.—R. TENBROECK, General Eastern Agent.
    J. F. WILEY, Passenger Agent.
    F. R. SEAMAN, City Passenger Agent.

Ogden, Utah.—Union Depot.—C. A. HENRY, Ticket Agent.

Omaha, Neb.—Ninth and Farnam streets.—J. B. FRAWLEY, Traveling Passenger Agent.
    HARRY P. DEUEL, 1,302 Farnam street. City Passenger and Ticket Agent.
    J. K. CHAMBERS, Depot Ticket Agent, Tenth and Marcy streets.

Philadelphia, Pa.—133 South Fourth street.—T. P. VAILLE, Traveling Passenger Agent.

Pittsburgh, Pa.—215 Wood street.—H. E. PASSAVANT, Traveling Freight and Passenger Agent.

Portland Oregon.—Corner First and Oak streets.—A. L. MAXWELL, General Passenger and
    Ticket Agent Oregon Railway and Navigation Company.

St. Louis, Mo.—13 South Fourth street.—J. F. AGLAR, General Agent Freight and Passenger
    Departments.
    E. R. TUTTLE, Traveling Passenger Agent.
    A. W. BARBOUR, City Passenger Agent.

St. Paul, Minn.—154 East Third street.—F. L. LYNDE, Traveling Passenger Agent.

Sacramento, Cal.—1,018 Second street.—C. L. HANNA, Traveling Passenger Agent.

Salt Lake City, Utah.—201 Main street,—J. V. PARKER, Division Freight and Passenger Agent.
    C. E. INGALLS, City Passenger Agent.

San Francisco, Cal.—1 Montgomery street.—D. W. HITCHCOCK, General Agent Freight
    and Passenger Departments.
    W. G. HOLCOMBE, Passenger Agent.

                J. A. S. Reed, General Traveling Agent, 191 South Clark street, Chicago.
                E. L. LOMAX, Assistant General Passenger and Ticket Agent, Omaha, Neb.
                J. S. TEBBETS, General Passenger and Ticket Agent, Omaha, Neb.

PULLMAN PALACE CAR RATES.

Subject to Change.

THE PULLMAN PALACE CAR COMPANY now operates this class of service on the Union Pacific and connecting lines.

PULLMAN PALACE CAR RATES BETWEEN	Double Berths.	Drawing Room.
New York and Chicago	$ 5.00	$ 18.00
New York and St. Louis	6.00	22.00
Chicago and Omaha or Kansas City	2.50	9.00
Chicago and Denver	6.00	21.00
St. Louis and Kansas City	2.00	7.00
St. Louis and Omaha	2.50	9.00
Kansas City and Cheyenne	4.50	16 00
Council Bluffs, Omaha or Kansas City and Denver	3.50	12.00
Council Bluffs or Omaha and Cheyenne	4.00	14.00
Council Bluffs, Omaha or Kansas City and Salt Lake	8.00	28.00
Council Bluffs, Omaha or Kansas City and Ogden	8.00	28.00
Council Bluffs, Omaha or Kansas City and Butte	9.50	36.00
Council Bluffs, Omaha or Kansas City and San Francisco or Los Angeles	13.00	50.00
Council Bluffs, Omaha or Kansas City and Portland	13.00	50.00
Cheyenne and Portland	10.00	38.00
Denver and Portland	10.00	38.00
Denver and Los Angeles	11.00	42.00
Denver and San Francisco	11.00	42.00
Denver and Leadville	2.00	....

For a Section, twice the Double Berth Rates will be charged.

The excursion, hotel, dining, hunting and sleeping cars of the Pullman Company will accommodate from 12 to 18 persons, allowing a full bed to each, and are fitted with such modern conveniences as private, observation and smoking rooms, folding beds, reclining chairs, buffets, and kitchens. They are especially arranged for tourists, theatrical companies, sportsmen, and private parties. The hunting cars have special conveniences, being provided with dog-kennels, gun-racks, fishing-tackle, lockers, etc. These cars can be chartered at following rates per diem (the time reckoned being from date of departure until return of same, unless otherwise arranged with the Pullman Company):

TEN DAYS OR LESS.

	PER DAY.		PER DAY.
Hotel cars	$ 50.00	Excursion or hunting cars	$ 35.00
Buffet cars	45.00	Excursion cars with buffet	30.00
Sleeping cars	40.00	Dining cars	30.00

OVER TEN DAYS—$5.00 per day less than above. Hotel, buffet, or sleeping cars can also be chartered for continuous trips without lay-over between points where extra cars are furnished (cars to be given up at destination), as follows:

Where berth rate is ....$1.50, car rate will be........ ....$35.00
"   "   "   .... 2.00, " " " 45.00
"   "   "   .... 2.50, " " " 55.00

For each additional berth rate of 50 cents, car rate will be increased $10.00.

Above rates include service of polite and skillful attendants, and a commissariat, if desired. Such chartered cars must contain not less than 15 persons holding first-class tickets, and another full-fare ticket will be required for each additional passenger over 15. If chartered " per diem" cars are given up en route, chartering party must arrange for return to original starting point free, or pay amount of freight necessary for return thereto. Diagrams showing interior of these cars can be had of any agent of the Pullman Company.

EXCURSION TICKETS AND RATES OF FARE.

Excursion tickets to prominent resorts west of the Missouri River are on sale during the summer months in most of the eastern cities at greatly reduced rates of fare. These tickets are good from ninety days to six months. Excursion tickets to San Francisco, California, and to Portland, Oregon, are on sale all the year around. From its Missouri River terminals—Council Bluffs, Omaha, St. Joseph, Leavenworth, and Kansas City—the Union Pacific Railway has placed on sale at greatly reduced rates, excursion tickets to all the prominent places and resorts on its lines in Colorado, Wyoming, Montana, Idaho, Oregon, and Utah; also excursion tickets for side trips have been placed on sale at greatly reduced rates during the summer months via the Union Pacific Railway at all its prominent places of resort in the above-mentioned territory. For large excursion parties to Idaho Springs, Shoshone Falls, Soda Springs, Garfield Beach, Great Salt Lake, and Utah Hot Springs, the Union Pacific Railway will make special excursion rates for side trips to prominent points of interest near these resorts.

BAGGAGE RATES.

Subject to Change.

Free baggage allowance on each full ticket of any class is 150 pounds, and on each half ticket 75 pounds, to railroad points, including San Francisco and all Pacific coast points, except between stations in Nebraska, where the free baggage allowance is 200 pounds on full tickets and 100 on half tickets. Baggage may be checked through from all points in the United States or Canada to Union Pacific Railway points, or beyond, including Pacific coast points. The Union Pacific was the first line west of the Missouri River to inaugurate this system.

Passengers holding full first-class tickets, issued on steamship orders sold in foreign countries, for transportation through the United States to foreign ports, in either direction, will be allowed 250 pounds of baggage free on each full ticket, and 125 pounds free on each half ticket.

Extra baggage rates, per 100 pounds, to local points on the Union Pacific and Oregon Railway & Navigation Company's lines, is 12 per cent. of first-class fare. Free baggage allowance on stages is from 30 to 50 pounds, and the charge for extra weight higher than for same distance by rail.

Members of the same family can pack their usual allowance of baggage in one or more trunks, provided no trunk exceeds 250 pounds in weight.

The extra baggage rate from Missouri River to points in California is $7.20 per 100 pounds on all classes of tickets.

GUNS.—Uncased guns will be carried in baggage car only, and no charge will be made for a distance of 100 miles or less. For distances over 100 miles, baggagemen may charge 25 cents for each passenger division. Cased guns will be checked free by baggage agents, as part of the usual baggage allowance, or they may be carried by passengers in coaches without charge.

FOR CARE OF DOGS.—Baggagemen will collect 25 cents per head for each division less than 100 miles, and for distances over 100 miles at the rate of one-quarter of a cent per mile.

BABY CARRIAGES—When accompanied by a passenger with an infant, may be carried by train baggagemen, and 25 cents collected for each passenger division, but when not so accompanied must be turned over to the express company.

BICYCLES AND TRICYCLES—Will be carried free in baggage cars, when accompanied by the owner, on presentation of a first-class ticket upon which no baggage has been checked.

MEALS.

All trains stop at regular eating stations, where first-class meals are furnished under the direct supervision of this company, by the Pacific Hotel Company. Neat and tidy lunch counters are also to be found at these stations.

BRANCHES AND AUXILIARY LINES COMPRISING THE SYSTEM.

NEBRASKA DIVISION.

	MILES.
Main Line.—Council Bluffs to Cheyenne	520.2
Omaha and Republican Valley Branch.—Valley to Beatrice, Kans., Valparaiso to Stromsburg, and Grand Island to Ord, St. Paul to Loup City	258.6
Omaha, Niobrara & Black Hills Branch.—Columbus, Neb., to Norfolk, Oconee to Albion, and Genoa to Cedar Rapids	114.5
Total, Nebraska Division	893.3

COLORADO DIVISION.

WYOMING DIVISION.

IDAHO DIVISION.

KANSAS DIVISION.

MILES.

Salt Lake & Western Division.—Lehigh Junction to Tintic and Silver City............ ... 53.8
Utah Central Division.—Ogden to Frisco, Junction to Syracuse.... ... . 285.5
Garfield Beach Branch Utah & Nevada Railway.—Salt Lake to terminus narrow gauge ... 37.0
Montana Union Railway.—Silver Bow, Butte, Garrison and Anaconda 59.6

RECAPITULATION.

Nebraska Division.......... .... 803.3
Colorado Division.. .... 584.3
Wyoming Division 682.9
Idaho Division....... ....1,019.7
Kansas Division.......... ....1,209.6
Salt Lake & Western Division................ .... 53.8
Utah Central Division.... .... 285.5
Montana Union Railway.......... .... 59.6
Utah & Nevada Railway, Garfield Beach Branch.... .... 37 0

Total............... ....5,125.7

NOTES.

TRAINS, EQUIPMENT, JUNCTIONS, AND CONNECTIONS.

IT is worth while knowing that two through trains leave Council Bluffs every day with through cars for Denver, Ogden, Salt Lake City, Los Angeles, San Francisco, and Portland. One of these trains, the fast one, called "The Overland Flyer," has Pullman Palace Sleeping Cars only, running through to Denver, Los Angeles, San Francisco, and Portland. The other train, the Overland Express has Pullman Palace Sleeping Cars, Modern Day Coaches, and Free Family Sleeping Cars. From Kansas City two fast express trains leave daily with through cars for Denver, Cheyenne, Salt Lake City, and Portland. These trains have Pullman Palace Sleeping Cars and Modern Day Coaches. The morning train has the Free Family Sleeping Cars. The equipment of these trains is unsurpassed and all that can be desired. A good roadbed, standard-gauge track, steel rails, iron bridges, and stone culverts combined, insure safety and speed.

The important points where connections are made are as follows:

JULESBURG, Colorado, five miles from the Colorado-Nebraska State line, where the Council Bluffs & Denver line branches off to Denver.

DENVER, Colorado, where the Colorado branches of the Union Pacific Railway connect for Idaho Springs, and important cities, resorts, and places in Colorado.

CHEYENNE, Wyoming, where the Kansas main line from Kansas City and the Denver Pacific main line from Denver to Cheyenne, join the Nebraska main line.

GRANGER, Wyoming, where the Oregon Short Line branches off to Huntington and Portland, Oregon. The trains, however, connect at Green River, thirty miles east of Granger, and are made up at that point.

POCATELLO, Idaho, where the Utah & Northern branch of the Union Pacific Railway connects with the main line for Butte, Garrison, and Helena. From Pocatello the Utah & Northern branch also diverges south to Ogden, Salt Lake City, and Garfield Beach.

BEAVER CAÑON, Idaho, on the Utah & Northern branch, where connection is made with Union Pacific stages for the Yellowstone National Park.

SHOSHONE STATION, Idaho, on the Oregon Short Line, where connection is made, via stage, for the great SHOSHONE FALLS, and also where a branch of the Oregon Short Line makes connection for Hailey and Ketchum.

NAMPA, Idaho, where the Idaho Central Railroad connects with the Oregon Short Line for Boise City.

HUNTINGTON, Oregon, where the junction of the Oregon Short Line branch of the Union Pacific Railway with the Oregon Railway & Navigation Company, an auxiliary line of the Union Pacific Railway, is made for Portland.

OGDEN, Utah, where the Utah Central branch of the Union Pacific Railway connects with the main line, for Salt Lake City, Garfield Beach, Provo, Spanish Forks and Frisco, and also where the Central Pacific Railroad connects for Sacramento, Los Angeles, and San Francisco.

SALT LAKE CITY, Utah, where the Utah & Nevada branch of the Union Pacific Railway connects for Garfield Beach, on the shores of the Great Salt Lake.

OUTLINE OF THE TRIP ACROSS THE CONTINENT.

Leaving Council Bluffs via the Nebraska main line, and Kansas City via the Kansas main line, the two lines join at Cheyenne. The Kansas main line runs to Denver; and the trip from Denver to Cheyenne along the foothills of the Rocky Mountains affords the tourist a kaleidoscopic panorama of hills, fields, rivers, running brooks, and lofty mountains. Leaving Cheyenne the summit of the Rockies is passed at Sherman, elvation 8,235 feet, the highest point on the transcontinental ride between the Missouri River and the Pacific coast. Leaving Sherman, Ames' Monument and Hippopotamus Rock can be seen from the windows of the car. Dale Creek bridge, a wonderful structure over Dale Creek, is passed. Then comes Rawlins, Rock Springs, and GREEN RIVER.

ROUTE TO PORTLAND, OREGON.

At GREEN RIVER the trains for Portland, Oregon, are made up, although they do not make their departure from the main line over the Oregon Short Line until Granger is reached, thirty miles west of Green River, and the trip across the continent is continued over the Oregon Short Line, reaching out, as it does, to the great Northwest. The road goes along over moderate curves and grades, through pretty little valleys along the Bear River, until the great

Territory of Idaho is entered at Border Station. Then on through Soda Springs and Pocatello—the junction with the Utah & Northern branch, for Butte, Garrison, and Helena; thence to Shoshone Station, where the junction is made for the great Shoshone Falls, via stage, and also for Hailey and Ketchum, via rail, over a branch of the Oregon Short Line ; thence from Shoshone Station the road stretches away through Nampa, where the junction is made with the Idaho Central for Boise City, nineteen miles distant ; thence on from Nampa, through Caldwell and Weiser to Huntington, just within Oregon, the terminus of the Oregon Short Line, where connection is made with the Oregon Railway & Navigation Company, one of the auxiliary lines of the Union Pacific Railway; thence from Huntington through Baker City, Union, La Grande, Pendleton, and Umatilla Junction to "The Dalles," which takes its name from the dalles of the Columbia. From this point on to East Portland the trip is one replete with scenic wonders. Arriving in Portland, which is the metropolis of the northwest Pacific coast, and a large, handsome, cosmopolitan city, the trip across the continent to Portland, Oregon, is complete, one of the grandest within the reach of the traveler.

From Portland, magnificent ocean steamers depart for the far distant Orient. Fine steamers also ply over the broad bosom of the Pacific Ocean from Portland to Alaska, that wonderful Territory of the North. The Oregon Railway & Navigation Company's steamers, which compare favorably with the Atlantic steamships, make regular trips twice a week from Portland to San Francisco.

ROUTE TO SAN FRANCISCO.

From GREEN RIVER, the trip across the continent to San Francisco is continued. Three miles west of Green River is Fish Cut. Green River Buttes are objects of interest, and are within sight for miles. After passing Granger, Evanston is soon reached. At Wasatch Station, the summit of the Wasatch range of mountains is reached. The elevation is 6,812 feet, and at this point the road enters Echo Cañon. Echo Creek, which runs through the cañon, is crossed thirty-one times in twenty-six miles. Three and a half miles west of Wasatch, the train runs into a tunnel 900 feet long. One mile east of Castle Rock is a queer formation of rock resembling the ruins of an old castle. " Hanging Rock " is what its name indicates. Two and a half miles west of Emory, on top of the bluff, is a rock called " Jack in the Pulpit," and further on can be seen the heights of Echo Cañon, on top of which are the old Mormon fortifications. Then comes "Steamboat Rocks." Just before reaching Echo are seen the "Amphitheatre," " Pulpit Rocks," and " Bromley's Cathedral." At Echo Station, Weber Cañon is entered. One and a half miles west of Echo can be seen the "Witch Rocks." Five miles further on is the 1,000-mile tree, and a mile further on is " Devil's Slide." Echo and Weber Cañons compare favorably with the celebrated Colorado cañons. Three and a half miles west of Corydon, the cañon broadens out, and to the left are noticed the first of the Mormon settlements. About one-half mile away, between Peterson and Uintah Station, " Devil's Gate " is to be seen, and shortly after the country widens into the Great Salt Lake Valley, when Ogden is reached. The first view of the valley after the surfeit of mountain scenery, is one of striking contrast, quiet and pleasant to the eye. Between Cheyenne and Ogden, about ten miles of snow sheds altogether are passed at different points on the line. These sheds are located between Granite Cañon and Buford, Buford and Sherman, Sherman and Dale Creek, Dale Creek and Harney, Wilcox and Aurora, Carbon and Simpson, Simpson and Percy, and Piedmont and Aspen, all in Wyoming. These sheds are quite a feature of the ride across the continent, the Central Pacific Railroad having about thirty miles altogether on its line between Ogden and Sacramento. Ogden is 1,034 miles from Council Bluffs and 833 miles from San Francisco; the trip to Salt Lake City and Garfield Beach is made from this point. From Ogden, the trip is made over the Central Pacific Railroad, over great plains and through immense snow sheds, great mountain ranges and jagged foothills, until Reno is reached.

Leaving Ogden, the train passes Promontory, which was intended to be the point of junction of the two roads forming the transcontinental route, namely, the Union and Central Pacific Railroads. Later, Ogden was decided upon as a compromise.

The crowning scenes of the trip across Utah, Nevada and California are not reached until Reno is passed. Cape Horn, Emigrant Gap, the Sierra Nevadas, Donner Lake and other objects of more than ordinary interest will be found. Nevada is celebrated for her famous mines. The great mines of Virginia City and the Sutro Tunnel attract numerous visitors. The marvelous Carson and Humboldt sinks, in which the waters of all the rivers in the State of Nevada save one are swallowed, the Mud Lakes, the Borax marshes, and countless numbers of thermal springs, have been the wonder of the scientist and the delight of the tourist. One hundred and fifty-five miles from Reno is Sacramento, a beautiful city, and the capital of California. It is delightfully located upon the east bank of the Sacramento River, in the midst of the most productive grain fields, vineyards, and orchards in the world. The climate is delightful, and the surrounding country entrancing.

From Sacramento, the Central Pacific Railroad branches off via Lathrop to Los Angeles, from which point the prominent cities and noted resorts of California are readily reached. From Sacramento, the Davis cut-off, now the main line of the Central Pacific road, takes the tourist through to Oakland, where a transfer is made across an arm of the bay to San Francisco, and here this part of the trip "Across the Continent" terminates at San Francisco, where old Sol, darkly red from his days' exertion, sinks to rest in the broad bosom of the Pacific Ocean.

COLORADO POINTS.

DENVER.

DENVER is the social and commercial centre, not alone of Colorado, but also of the outlying Territories, and is called the "Queen City of the Plains." Its elevation is 5,203 feet above the sea-level. It is the gate to the mineral and scenic phenomena that have made the Rocky Mountains famous. In addition to its other advantages, it has a peerless climate, more conducive to outdoor enjoyment than any other known locality. It is situated on the plains at the foot, and almost within the shadow, of the "Mighty Hills," which protect it alike from the extremes of summer and winter weather. The streets are long and level, and on either side are rows of shade trees—nourished by streams of running water—casting a shade alike upon the mansion and the cottage. There is not a paved street in the city, nor one in which the natural roadway has been improved, and there is no other city whose thoroughfares are as smooth and solid. Its hotels are excellent; in fact they have all the improvements and modern conveniences possessed by the large hotels in the East, and the best ones would be first class even in Chicago, St. Louis, New York, or Boston.

From Denver there is an unbroken view of the Rocky Mountains for nearly three hundred miles, reaching from beyond Long's Peak on the north to the historical summit of Pike's Peak on the south. This lovely mountain view is an everyday affair to the citizens of Denver, but nowhere in the world can its beauty and grandeur be surpassed.

The Union Pacific Railway runs two solid trains each way daily between Council Bluffs and Denver, and two solid trains each way daily between Kansas City and Denver.

IDAHO SPRINGS.

Idaho Springs, 7,567 feet above the sea-level, is a beautiful place located in Clear Creek Cañon. It is reached from Denver, via Golden, on the Colorado Central branch of the Union Pacific Railway.

In so far as nature equips resorts, Idaho Springs is the finest that the Rocky Mountains afford. It is thirty-eight miles from Denver, situated in a cup, as it were, formed by the receding, half-encircling sides of the cañon. The heights on either side are not rocky and rugged, but verdant and inviting. Sometimes deer are seen wandering through them, almost within sight of the hotels. The place has a population of over 2,000 people, and some of the cottages cling to the sides of the cañon in a very unique and perplexing manner. The roads are level and smooth and lead to the most delightful retreats. The hotels are good, and society the best. Idaho Springs is so near Denver that many families from the latter city summer here, stopping either at its excellent hotels or at the adjoining cottages.

The springs themselves are a great attraction, resting the wearied and healing the sick. Hot and steaming they bubble and hiss from the ground, or icy cool they rise to the surface, and steal away in glassy streams. Besides the numerous private baths, there is also a mammoth swimming bath, in which a good swim may be enjoyed, as a current from the earth's bosom is continually flowing. The natural cavern, hot as a Turkish bathroom, is more effective than that penetrating bath. It boils impurities from the blood and aches from the bones. There seems to be life in it. The pool that the angel troubled in olden times never worked greater curative wonders.

People drink the cool water with the same zest that they bathe in the warm, and with equally good results. It has everything that the delicate require, such as pure air, constant sunshine, and invigorating waters. An experienced and traveled physician has started a sanitarium at Idaho Springs, selecting it because it has more days of sunshine in a year than any place within his knowledge.

The following is an analysis of its hot waters :

Carbonate of soda	52.81
Carbonate of lime	16.32
Carbonate of magnesia	4.94
Carbonate of iron	7.07
Sulphate of soda	50.34
Sulphate of magnesia	32.09
Chloride of sodium	7.13
Silicate of soda	6.99
Total	177.69

CLEAR CREEK CAÑON.

Clear Creek Cañon is one of the wildest gorges in Colorado. Through the solid rock of this gorge has been blasted the roadbed of the Union Pacific Railway. It is the most accessible gorge of any in the State. In the days of stages and freight-wagons, it was used as a thoroughfare. The cañon is only about one hour's ride from Denver, and it is reached from this city, via Golden, by the Colorado Central branch of the Union Pacific Railway. This division of the Union Pacific Railway, until it reaches the foothills, lies through fields as green and farmhouses as pleasant as any that the older States can boast of.

Leaving Denver Union Depot, the road winds along past Argo and Arvada to Golden, a pretty and thrifty place just fairly in the mountains. Its site is the bed of an ancient lake, which has left its smooth-washed boulders and water marks, the latter high in the air along the buttes. The road enters the cañon a few miles west of Golden, and continues on up to Silver Plume and Graymont. Branching off at Forks Creek, where the passenger trains divide, one section hurries onward up to Central City along a branch of Clear Creek Cañon, while the other continues along the cañon to Georgetown.

The cañon is a marvelous cliff worn through the solid rock by Clear Creek, dashing and roaring near the track, which crosses it at short intervals. Its sides, timeworn into a thousand grotesque forms, rise from 500 to 1,500 feet, making the sky look like a narrow strip. In places there are intersecting gullies, through which rivulets come silvering down, and the sunlight strikes across the sombre cañon Trees grow thick in places, and crown a portion of the heights. At Beaver Brook there is a pavilion for dancing, and other accommodations for picnickers.

From Forks Creek the railway branches off to Blackhawk and Central City, two towns really merging into one. They are but little over a mile apart in actual distance, yet to reach Central City from Blackhawk the train passes over four miles of marvelously constructed track, passing, as it rises, by the dumps of famous mines, and above crushing and grinding mills. From Central City there is a good stage line to Idaho Springs, so that these springs are also accessible from Central City, and the journey affords a view seldom surpassed.

From Forks Creek the road winds along the main cañon, through Idaho Springs to Georgetown. This town is built on silver-bearing soil, and is surrounded on three sides by the mountains. It is strange to see this town of 4,000 people, an animated gem in the setting of the Rockies, with long, roomy, stoneless streets and handsome residences. It has an altitude of 8,500 feet—considered an ideal height by many. Georgetown seems at first to be the end of Clear Creek Cañon, but there is an opening beyond, and through it the road has forced its way.

Green Lake is an emerald gem, sparkling in the sunlight, two miles away from Georgetown, and 2,000 feet higher. The lake is clear as crystal, but the basin that holds it is green, the sand in it is green, and the moss festoons it like a green veil. In places its depth is unknown, and its feeding springs have never been found. In its depths the gaunt limbs of skeleton trees, dead but erect, beckon from below the ripples on its surface, while trout glide through the branches where once the songster of the forest plumed its wings. At one end of the lake is the Battle Ground of the Gods, where, according to Indian legends, great boulders lie as the wrath of warring deities hurled them. Some of the largest of these have formed the Cave of the Winds, through which the breezes dolefully sigh.

After leaving Georgetown, the chief point of interest is "The Loop," and here it is that the real glories of the trip are appreciated. The mind can readily understand how a train may wind through a chasm. It is less easy, however, to realize how, beginning to rise along the side, the elevation continues until the tourist looks down upon a town, as it were in miniature. Continuing on its tortuous course, the train worms its way up a steep grade, carved and blasted through the rock, and skirts the sides of the mountains that lose their crests in snow. In the valley flows the little stream of Clear Creek. Past Devil's Gate and Bridal Veil Falls the engine curves and climbs. Looking directly above, a railroad track is seen on a high iron bridge over-spanning the track almost at right angles, but in the form of a crescent. The tourist wonderingly inquires, "What road is that above and how did it get there?" For a little way the track is comparatively straight; then it varies to the right, crosses the creek and starts down the valley, but still going up grade. For perhaps a quarter of a mile this continues. Then the creek is crossed again on a high iron bridge. Looking directly down, a track is seen below. Then the tourist wonders what track that is and how it got there. He looks again before satisfying himself that it is the same track he just passed over. He is now on the bridge up to which he was looking but a moment ago. He then realizes that he has just ridden over an immense loop—one of four in existence. There is one on the Southern Pacific, one in Switzerland, and one in the Andes of South America, but this is the most complex of them all. The bridge just crossed is 300 feet long and 86 high. From Georgetown it can be seen one way, nestled in the mountains; looking at it from the other way there seems to be nothing but a confusion of tracks.

It is a remarkable climb from here to the Big Fill, which is seventy-six feet high, but too sharp a curve to admit of a bridge, and comes near being a duplication of the "The Loop." Georgetown is still in sight beyond the three parallel tracks of "The Loop." Looking down the final curve there is a wealth of track, but it dodges hither and thither, no portion, seemingly, having any special relation to its neighbor ; occasionally the entire trackage comes into view at once.

After passing "The Loop" and Silver Plume, Graymont, the terminus of the railway, is reached. The tourist must not neglect to make this trip, as it is one of the most celebrated in America.

PLATTE CAÑON.

Twenty miles from Denver, on the South Park branch, is Platte Cañon, and through this sinuous rift in the mountains rushes the Platte River, dancing out of its shadowy channel into the full light of the valley. The

South Park branch of the Union Pacific Railway, which is the short line to Leadville and the Gunnison country, enters the cañon where the river leaves it. The general aspect is much like that of Clear Creek Cañon, and it is a friendly rival. It is the same in being a rocky chasm, its bed a rushing stream, but different in its wild contour. To reach Platte Cañon, the trains on the South Park division of the Union Pacific Railway pass through the western suburbs of Denver, skirting the wooded banks of the Platte, and twenty miles out, just where the river dances into the sunlight, enter the gloomy cañon between lofty and forbidding walls, which continue for fifty miles, receeding at times to make room for picturesque little hamlets like Buffalo, Pine Grove, Cassells, Slaghts, and Grant. At all of these places tourists can be accommodated and trout and game abound.

At times the train seems about to dash against the face of the cliff, but following the heavy steel rails, it turns suddenly and passes by in safety. The way through the cañon is a series of graceful curves, close to the overhanging rocks, often crossing the turbulent Platte River. In places the tops of the cañon almost seem to touch and exclude the sun. The cañon is a geological study ; the different formations and the terrific force which have combined them tell their own stories.

Dome Rock is like the top of a buried mosque and is as regular in shape as if fashioned by the hand of man, except that one side is partly broken away. Cathedral Spires are in sight for miles, despite the winding of the cañon, and keep reappearing long after they are passed.

This cañon affords fine opportunities for camping out. There is shade in plenty, trout, game, and bathing, and good board to be had at neighboring houses. But the best way is to live in a tent, and hire a servant to do the cooking. This is especially commended to the invalid tourist. There are fifty miles of this varying panorama, and after the train climbs Kenosha Hill, South Park is seen stretching away, one vast and level picture, as different from the cañon as night is from day.

BOULDER CAÑON.

Boulder Cañon is reached from Denver via the Colorado Central branch of the Union Pacific Railway to Boulder. From Boulder a narrow-gauge road has been built into Boulder Cañon by the Union Pacific Railway. This cañon can favorably compare with Clear Creek and Platte Cañons, yet it does not equal them in length, massiveness, nor height. In one place, a perfect image of Minnehaha comes dashing down from amid evergreen sides, and this spot has long been a rendezvous for picnic excursions.

The road, on leaving the town of Boulder, passes through a beautiful grove, and continues on by Baldwin, Four Mile Cañon, and Gold Hill, until it reaches Penn's Gulch, now known as Sunset. Just before arriving at Sunset, an upward glance reveals the high range of mountains, but passing that, the ascent is much like that of Kenosha Hill in the South Park, affording, if possible, a much finer view. It's a glorious mount of the range, with sweeping, rock-bound curves, each one bringing the visitor nearer the summit. The valley, with its wavering hills, is receding. The view from the summit is pronounced by Mr. Jackson the finest in Colorado. The end of the curve is seven and a half miles from Sunset. In that distance there is a marvelous rise of many feet. The end of this grade, after all its meanderings, is visible from Sunset. Sunset is an acquisition to the excursionist ; Boulder was good before, but with the new adjunct, is doubly so. The altitude of Sunset is 7,731 feet. The view around Sunset is glorious. On every hand the mountains are glistening with snow. Peak rises above peak with majesty unspeakable ; yet wearying of these, the eye may turn and be rested by the vastness of the plains and the intervening hills.

Boulder is forty-seven miles from Denver on the broad-gauge Colorado Central, a branch of the Union Pacific Railway, although the cut-off via Argo and C. C. junctions make it only twenty-nine miles. It can also be reached from Denver via Golden or via Brighton. Its altitude is 5,331 feet, and it has a population of over 4,000. It has good hotels and is a fine summering place. Boulder is the county seat of Boulder County, and a key to the cañon of the same name. It is situated just at the junction of the foothills with the plains, thus enjoying the cool breezes from the mountains, while on the other hand stretch away green and fertile acres for cattle and crops. Underneath these acres are vast deposits of coal and precious metals, which combine to make Boulder an important mining centre. Within a few miles of the town are many pretty lakes, dotted with water-fowl. The Seltzer Springs, of Springdale, are ten miles northwest. The waters from these springs are steadily growing in popularity, and are among the best mineral waters in Colorado. Along Jim Creek is the attractive little glen in which they are found, amidst a dense forest of pines, through which runs a fine carriage road. Stages run daily from Boulder to this point, where there are good hotels and excellent accommodations.

GRAY'S PEAK.

Gray's Peak is reached from Denver through Clear Creek Cañon, via Golden, Forks Creek, Idaho Springs, Georgetown, and Silver Plume to Gray-mont, the terminus of the railway, from which station the ascent must be made.

This peak is hidden by intervening mountains from the view at Graymont, the station where horses are taken for its ascent. There is a cozy little hotel here, with plenty of safe horses and guides, but the trail is so easy that a child could almost lead the way. Gray's is higher than Pike's or Long's Peak, and Blanca only exceeds it by a few feet in height. Mounting after breakfast, after a sharp turn to the left, an earnest climb begins that continues over ridge and wooded gullies for two miles. The road has now dwindled to a path. On the left are abrupt heights, to which cling the lonely cabins of miners. The tunnels above them appear to have no greater circumference than rabbit holes. The trail leads across grassy-banked rivulets and blooming knolls past Kelso Mountain; then, rounding the hill, Gray's Peak looms up unobscured for the first time. Gray's Peak is not rough and chasmed, but its vastness seems all the greater, for the reason that it has preserved such a geological calm, and now, like a monarch, mighty in its superiority, looks down upon its fellows, sending the morning shadow of its greatness far on to the Pacific slope, and its evening profile toward the remote Atlantic. It is a mass, dread and awful. The air is rare and clear. Snow is piled about in eternal drifts, and below each drift, drawing its life from the exuding dampness, is a bed of flowers. Strange anomaly! Winter's hoary locks decked with the buds of June. Vegetation is soon left behind, except here and there a hardy plant, rooted in the rocks. The trail ahead is seen on a series of inclined plains to the very crest, going backward and forward, but always rising. The hills and cliffs, which seemed so lofty, are now far below, and the lesser mountains are left behind, the only one unconquered being Gray's Peak. A wavering line stretches back to the valley, and the tourist wonders vaguely if that is the trail he has just come over. The horse pants as he takes the last turn, his shoes clink upon the granite jewels of the continental crown, and Gray's Peak is beneath you. The sea is 14,441 feet below your level. Hats off! The Genius of this sublime solitude demands homage.

They who have traversed the globe say that it affords but one such prospect. A pictured landscape so mighty in conception that it overpowers, yet harmonious as an anthem in all its infinite diffusion of color and form, framed only by the limit of the eye's vision—a picture where the lakes gleam and the rivers flow—where the trees nod and the cloud-ships clash in mystic collision with the peaks that have invaded their realm, while the moving sun floods it with real life and warmth.

That which is beheld in silence, who shall describe? Below is the kingly monument meeting the heavens and declaring with them the glory of God. In every direction spurs of the Rocky Mountains bewilder the eye till remoteness swallows them up. Pike's Peak is a neighbor; Lincoln's and Long's seem near. The smoke of a score of towns is seen. Every park in the State may be located. Rivers are traced from source to mouth. Eastward are the plains— a waterless ocean—each town a fleet, each house a sail, each grove an island. A dozen peaks over 14,000 feet high are seen. The Holy Cross, like a sacred seal, glints in the sunlight miles and miles away. The Uintah Mountains, in Utah, are faint but distinct; and so are the Spanish Peaks, which keep watch at the line between Colorado and New Mexico. To see the sun rise here is a tourist's triumph. To do this, Graymont must be left at 1 o'clock a. m.

Scaling the path by moonlight, fording noisy and dimly seen streams, or plunging into the darkness of the pines, is a novel experience. Gradually the stars fade out and Gray's Peak, the grim, granite monarch, shines with a borrowed luster, giving back faintly the glow of coming morning. A thousand mountains turn rosy before Aurora's approach, and then burst into a radiance of responsive greeting as she asserts full sway. The valley below is covered up in darkness, for the light that quenced the stars has not yet fallen upon it. The landscape, at first but a vast expanse without shape or limit, resolves itself into an army of mountains, gathered in stupendous array about the Dome of the Continent.

Imagine a view such as the flying bird has—seen with human vision—which comprehends the true and the beautiful, whether found in the realm of nature or of art. Imagine the heavens divinely painted; the earth striving to give back its color; the concourse of peaks meeting the clouds, and the valleys stretching between developing upon the sight, such as the image thrown by a monster stereopticon, as the morning light comes over the heights upon this scene.

Gray's Peak is Colorado's finest attraction. It is the highest point accessible by horse, and commands the most unapproachable view.

POINTS ABOUT THE COLORADO PARKS.

To fully understand the Colorado parks they must be seen. No description can do them justice, and neither the skill of a Bierstadt or Moran could picture their pure atmosphere—so like a breath from paradise—nor reproduce their beauteous colors and forms. In the city a park is a huge square, with trees in checker-board primness, where

> The sign, "Keep off the Grass,"
> Is enforced by policemen in blue and brass.

The lakes have fish as tame as chickens; the animals are in cages, and are neither attractive nor natural! But how different a mountain park! The range kindly parts to give it room, and shields it in its great arms. There are grassy hills and dales where feed the noblest game, and trees which shelter birds of plumage and song. The lakes—some of them miles in length—are rippled by the coming and going of ducks and geese. The streams bear along, eager for the bait of the angler, their speckled loads of trout, most delicious as they brown over the evening's coals. There are no precise graveled walks, and no elaborate fountains, but the footfall is lost on the turf, and springs gush forth with sparkling tune to gladden the thirsty with a liquid such as never ran through the rusty pipes of a city. The altitude gives coolness without chill, and warmth without oppressive heat.

ESTES PARK.

Estes Park is easily reached from Denver, via Loveland, on the Denver, Arkins & Fort Collins branch of the Union Pacific Railway, and a stage line which runs daily, except Sunday, from Loveland to the park.

Estes Park is pronounced the most beautiful of Colorado parks. It lies about sixty miles from Denver, at the foot of Long's Peak. The park is ten miles square, and its elevation is 8,000 feet above the sea-level. It is a wild and incomparable spot. Dinner is taken at Rattlesnake Park about noon, after a drive over one of the most beautiful and picturesque of mountain roads. The park is reached about 5 o'clock in the afternoon. The stage ride itself, with its beautiful views, is alone worth the trip. At one point on the line over thirty-five lakes on the plains and among the foothills are in view from the coach.

From the top of Bald Mountain and Pole Hill views can be had of the valleys of the Cache La Poudre, Big Thompson, and St. Vrain. The view of Estes Park and Snowy Range from Park Hill, just before descending into the park, is one of the grandest scenes in the Rocky Mountains. There are plenty of accommodations of every kind, and prices are reasonable. There are beautiful glades and odorous pines, numerous lakes, and game and trout in plenty.

NORTH PARK.

North Park is reached from Denver, via the Denver, Arkins & Fort Collins branch of the Union Pacific Railway to Fort Collins, a thrifty and attractive little town seventy-seven miles from Denver, and by stage from Fort Collins to the park. North Park can also be reached by stage from Laramie, Wyoming, on the main line of the Union Pacific Railway. The road from Fort Collins to the park goes through the world-famous Cache La Poudre region, where the hunting and fishing can not be excelled. North Park is Colorado's best hunting field. It is rugged in places, and vast. Its dimensions are seventy-five by fifty miles, with an elevation of 9,000 feet above the sea-level. The jagged spires of the Rockies, clothed with perpetual snow, look down upon the park from an elevation of some 14,000 feet. There are mineral springs, in stony basins, bubbling up icy cool from an unknown depth. In autumn the larger game comes down to join the grouse, quail, squirrel, and rabbit. A summer in North Park can be very pleasantly spent.

MIDDLE PARK.

Middle Park is best reached from Denver, via the Colorado Central branch of the Union Pacific Railway, through Georgetown or Sunset, and by stage from either place to the park. The road from Georgetown, however, is the best and most generally preferred. It is a notable ride by rail and stage.

Middle Park is like North Park, only larger, with more and larger hills and wider dales and streams of grander sweep.   The elevation is about 8,000 feet. From Georgetown to Hot Sulphur Springs is forty-six miles, just a day's journey.   This is the scenic centre of the park.   Never had nymphs of the wood a bathing place more charming.   The water is hot or cold, clear or sulphur charged.   Lave in its waters, and the aches and pains which flesh is heir to rapidly disappear.   The slopes of the Grand, Fraser, Blue, and Troublesome mountains, abound in feathered and other game.   Elk in particular are plenty.

SOUTH PARK.

South Park is best reached from Denver, via the Denver & South Park branch of the Union Pacific Railway to Kenosha, seventy-six miles from Denver, or to Como, eighty-eight miles from Denver.   Both of these places are in the park, and there are stage lines to different points of interest.   The park is about fifty miles in length and from ten to twenty miles in width, and its elevation is about 10,000 feet above the level of the sea.   South Park is in itself a magnificent domain.   It is not so rugged as the other parks, being more of a level plateau.   It is bordered on the east by a heavily timbered range some 2,000 feet above the park, while to the west the Snowy Range extends as far as the eye can reach.   In this range, in plain view, are a number of the highest peaks in Colorado.   One of the most noted mountains is the Mount of the Holy Cross, which can be seen from Robinson Station, a few miles from Leadville.   This is one of Colorado's wonders.   The elevation of this mountain is 14,176 feet above the sea-level.

Quoting from Mr. Ernest Ingersoll : " It is the Mount of the Holy Cross, bearing the sacred symbol in such heroic characters as dwarf all human graving, and set on the pinnacle of the world as though in sign of possession forever. The Jesuits went hand in hand with the *Chevalier Dubois*, proclaiming Christian Gospel in the northern forests ; the Puritan brought his Testament to New England; the Spanish banners of victory on the golden shores of the Pacific were upheld by the fiery zeal of the friars of San Francisco ; the frozen Alaskan cliffs resounded to the chanting of the monks of St. Peter and St. Paul.   On every side the virgin continent was taken in the name of Christ, and with all the eclat of religious conquest.   Yet from ages unnumbered before any of them, centuries oblivious in the mystery of past time, the cross had been planted here.   As a prophecy during unmeasured generations, as a sign of glorious fulfillment during nineteen centuries, from always and to eternity a reminder of our fealty to heaven, this divine seal has been set upon our proudest eminence."

This wonderful park can be seen from the line of the South Park branch of the Union Pacific Railway for a distance of nearly forty miles.   The road just skirts the park, so that the view extends clear over it. South Park is soft in coloring, magnificent in its sweep of distance, clothed in summer's velvet, trimmed with the ermine of never-melting snow, shaded by promontory, and flecked by countless herds of cattle. It is one of nature's masterpieces, and to those who love the quiet of beauty rather than its ruggedness, nothing will be found more impressive.

ALPINE TUNNEL.

Alpine Tunnel is on the line of the South Park branch of the Union Pacific Railway between St. Elmo and Gunnison. Leaving St. Elmo for Gunnison, the little town of Hancock is passed, and then a long, slanting tangent leads to a lofty hole in the mountain. On a little farther, and a plunge is taken into the blackness of Alpine Tunnel, shooting through the rocks at a height of 11,623 feet. Snow lies in perpetual banks on either side, but flowers bright and fragrant fill the frosty air with their perfume, and light it with their colors. Somewhere along the way the seasons clasp hands; for, though it be summer in the valley, it is not summer here — only that these flowery tokens sweetly defy the nipping chill. Except in the South American Andes, this tunnel is the highest railroad point ever attained. The tourist enters from the Atlantic slope, and emerges upon the Pacific. The point of change is in the centre, and the impetus tells the moment it is crossed. The engine, just before goaded to its work, has now to be held in severe check by the engineer. Two drops of water, such as continually fall from the roof, are hanging but half an inch apart. Trembling in the cold and blackness, they loosen their tiny hold and patter down. They were neighbors; but after hesitating a second, each starts with its fellows, and when they finally reach the ocean there is the span of a continent between them. The actual length of the tunnel, aside from its approaches, is 1,773 feet. The 70,000 linear feet of California redwood lining was brought up on pack horses over trails which had known the touch of no hoof save that of the mountain sheep, and where man himself had scarce dared to venture. Operations were carried on from both ends, and despite the curvature, when the respective gangs first caught the flash of the other's lamps, they were less than one inch out of the line the engineer had mapped out for them. The great expense was only warranted by the greatness of the country, which is now fastened to the outer world by this link of darkness. After passing the tunnel, on the way to Gunnison, the Palisades, Quartz Valley, San Juan, Uncompaghre, Hair Pin Curve, and Juanita Hot Springs are objects of interest which the tourist should see.

LEADVILLE.

Leadville is best reached from Denver over the South Park division of the Union Pacific Railway, and from there the distance is 151 miles. The altitude of Leadville is 10,200 feet above the level of the sea.   The climate in winter is much milder than that of the Middle or Eastern States.   The population is over 20,000.   Leadville is one of the largest mining camps in the world, and within a decade, has grown from a mere cluster of miners' cabins to a cosmopolitan city possessing all the conveniences of an older place, with gas, electric lights, fine business blocks, elegant private residences, churches, banks, theatres, and good hotels.   In fact, Leadville is one of the wonders of the nineteenth century.   A visit to Colorado without a sight of Leadville is incomplete, as there is much to inspect in the noted mines and smelters, aside from the charming scenery.   Evergreen Lakes are readily reached by a stage drive of six miles over a good road, and Twin Lakes are also accessible.

GUNNISON.

Gunnison is a busy little city of 3,000 souls.   Its coal supplies are inexhaustible, while gold and silver underlie its hills.   As the site for immense steel works, its future is assured.   Already it boasts of gas and water works, and such a hotel as would be first class in any city.   Gunnison is a good rendezvous for hunting and fishing parties.

COLORADO EXCURSIONS.

Colorado resorts situated on the line of the Denver & Rio Grande Railroad, such as Manitou, Colorado Springs, Poncha Hot Springs, Durango, Wagon Wheel Gap, Salida, and Pueblo, can also be reached over the Union Pacific Railway, from Kansas City or Council Bluffs to Denver and thence by the Denver & Rio Grande Railroad.

Below is a partial list of excursions which may be made over the Colorado Central and South Park branches of the Union Pacific Railway from Denver.

COLORADO CENTRAL DIVISION.

Idaho Springs and return.
Boulder and return.
Sunset and return.
Estes Park and return, via Loveland and stage.
Middle Park and return, via Georgetown and stage to Hot Sulphur Springs—one day's ride each way.
Central City and return.
Central City to Idaho Springs and return, via stage from Central City to Idaho Springs, or vice versa.
Georgetown and return, taking in Devil's Gate, Bridal Veil, and Green Lake.
Graymont and return.

Gray's Peak and return, via Graymont, from which place horses and guides can be had to the summit.

North Park and return, via Loveland and stage.

SOUTH PARK DIVISION.

Points as far as Webster and return. Delightful fishing is found along the Platte Cañon and accommodations at every stopping place.

Kenosha and return.   Trains pass at Kenosha, overlooking South Park 10,000 feet above the level of the sea.

South Park and return, via Kenosha.

Breckinridge and return, taking in Como and Boreas. Boreas has an altitude of 11,498 feet.

Leadville and return.

Buena Vista and return.

Pitkin and return, passing Alpine Tunnel, 11,623 feet above the sea.

Gunnison and return

COMBINATION ROUTES.

Leadville, over the South Park branch of the Union Pacific Railway, and return via the Denver & Rio Grande Railroad.

Gunnison, over the South Park branch of the Union Pacific Railway, and return via the Denver & Rio Grande Railroad.

Special excursion rates of about two cents per mile are made to cover these trips.

WYOMING POINTS.

WYOMING was organized as a Territory under an act of Congress passed July 25, 1868, and derives its name from the historical Wyoming Valley, of Pennsylvania, the scene of a barbarous massacre just after the American Revolution of 1776.

This Territory is as yet but sparsely settled, yet in natural resourses it is behind no section of America. It has broad, fertile acres, inexhaustible coal mines, is rich in minerals, stone, soda, oil, and timber. The tourist who passes through it must not base his judgment on the view from the car window. Remember that Yellowstone National Park itself is in Wyoming. There are soda lakes near Laramie and Rawlins, immense hot springs near Camp Ground, and warm springs near Fort Steele. For the hunter it is an ideal hunting ground, containing all manner of game, from cotton-tails to grizzly bears.

CHEYENNE.

Cheyenne, 6,038 feet in altitude, with a population of about 10,000, is one of the sprightliest and most prosperous cities in the entire West. It is well and compactly built, and for many years has been the centre of the cattle industry of the Northwest. Cheyenne has been a wild town, but is now a well regulated city with many fine stores and handsome residences. It constituted, for a long time, the outpost of civilization, becoming embodied in the legends of border life, and is a place of rare historical interest. Five miles from the city is Fort Russel, one of the largest military posts in the West.

SHERMAN,

A small station just west of Cheyenne, at an elevation of 8,235 feet, is the loftiest point in the transcontinental ride. From Sherman can be seen Long's

Peak, nearly 200 miles away, and the Ames' Monument, a pyramidal granite structure sixty-five feet in height, with a base of sixty feet square, which was erected by the Union Pacific Company to the memory of the Ames Brothers, to whom the completion of the Union Pacific Railway was largely due. Hippopotamus Rock is one of the sights of the vicinity. The scenery is wild and rugged. Just beyond Sherman is Dale Creek bridge, one of the most remarkable sights of the overland trip. The structure is of iron, and stretches from bluff to bluff with a 650-foot span. The train passes over it just 127 feet above the creek, which looks like a mere rivulet below. Pike's Peak can be seen away off to the south, not less than 165 miles distant. The Red Buttes, an object of interest to the tourist, lie just beyond.

LARAMIE.

Laramie, often called the "Gem City of the Rockies," has an elevation of 7,137 feet above sea-level, and a population of about 6,000. It is one of the principal towns on the main line of the Union Pacific Railway between Council Bluffs and Ogden. It is situated on Big Laramie River, fifty-seven miles northwest of Cheyenne, and is an important market for wool. Its schools are good, and the University of Wyoming and the United States Penitentiary are located here. Just southeast of the town is located the Territorial fish hatchery, at Soldier Springs. This has a capacity of hatching half a million trout at a time, and with these the streams and lakes of Wyoming are being rapidly stocked with the finest food-fish in the world. From Laramie there is a stage line, during the summer months, to North Park, Colorado.

GREEN RIVER.

There are many objects of interest in and around Green River, among which are the peculiar clay buttes, by which it is surrounded. The coal mines of Rock Springs and Carbon, a few miles east of Green River, are well worth a visit from the tourist. The quality of the coal is excellent, and is used by the Union Pacific Railway on its engines. It is at this point that the trains are made up for Portland, Oregon, although they do not leave the main line until Granger is reached, a few miles farther west.

EVANSTON.

Evanston, just west of Laramie, is another prosperous town, with a population of about 3,000 people, and an elevation of 6,747 feet above the sea-level. There is in this locality much to interest the hunter, the tourist, and the scientist. It is not far to the resorts of large game. The formation of the country is a peculiar one, it being broken, distorted, and worn into the most fantastic shapes. There are strong indications of precious metals, and a great wealth of coal and building materials. Near Evanston are a series of cool mineral springs that gush forth from a stratum of limestone with an abundant flow. Evanston is also a military post.

YELLOWSTONE NATIONAL PARK.

The park occupies the northwestern corner of Wyoming, extending slightly into Idaho and Montana. It is readily reached from Pocatello, by the Utah & Northern division of the Union Pacific Railway, via Beaver Cañon, Idaho, and thence by stage to Fire Hole Basin, in the park. Near Beaver Cañon are the Three Tetons overlooking Yellowstone Park, keeping, as it were, silent guard from their lofty heights over the National gift.

When Yellowstone National Park was set aside to be forever the grand tourist resort of the people, and their common property, few had an idea of the endless variety and stupendous grandeur of the features embraced in this tract of country, fifty-five by sixty-five miles. The park embraces an area of 3,000 square miles, has an average elevation of about 8,000 feet above sea-level, and is encircled by magnificent mountain ranges.

From Beaver Cañon the Union Pacific runs a fine line of stages to Fire Hole Basin, in the park, 100 miles distant. The stage ride from Beaver Cañon to Fire Hole Basin lies through a series of wonders, passing by Henry Lake, with its grassy shores that lie 3,000 feet below the peaks reflected in it. Sawtelle Mountain is full of darkly splendid caves. Cliff Lake is ten miles away. The plummet has been dropped 1,400 feet into its depths but found no bottom. Hunting and fishing in this vicinity will amply repay the sportsman, though he comes from over the ocean. Bowling over Tyghee Pass and into the luxuriant meadows of the Upper Madison Valley, the tourist overlooks a wilderness of pine-clothed heights and depths. Fifteen miles and the South Fork of the Madison River is crossed, a mile from the entrance of the park; once inside of which, the tourist is on Madison Terrace, a beautiful natural drive. There the tourist strikes a spur of Madison Range for Fire Hole Basin, from which roads reach to every attraction the park affords. From the summit there is another of these matchless views, including Madison Basin and the river as it winds for thirty miles in and out of sight. From Fire Hole Basin there are seen pillars of clouds showing where the springs and geyers are. Geyser Meadows are two miles away. Here are several geysers which throw their torrents twenty-five feet, or higher. Dome Spring is at the top of a calcareous deposit of livid colors, and some of its neighbors are similarly situated. "Queen Laundry" is a spring, whose waters will almost instantly cleanse even the dirtiest saddle blanket, and which finally drop into a basin at delightful bathing temperature. Fairy Creek Falls jump 250 feet over an adjacent cliff. With these spouting, leaping novelties all about, Midway Geyser Basin is reached five miles from Fire Hole Basin. Here are the grandest hot springs in the world. The overflow of hot water comes from the Great Spring, the equal of which no human eye ever saw. This aperture is 250 feet across and is walled in by sides thirty feet high. The surface is in constant turmoil, and the rising steam scalds the incautious. A glance into the gulf causes a shudder. Only a few yards away there is a cold fount twenty-five feet in diameter, filling an elaborately chased basin of unknown depth. Near by are the Chalk Vats, bubbling and spurting their mushy compound, and throwing out splashes of it which vary from a snowy white to a bright pink.

Upper Geyser Basin, ten miles from Fire Hole Basin, is the seat of the ten largest geysers ever discovered, beside which those of Iceland are trifling. There is a charming grove within a stone's throw of Castle Geyser, which begins to give vent to its pent up force in muttered thunder, and then its flood shoots over the cone, first a spurt, then a stream; then, with a shaking of the earth and a roar of a tempest, a river bounds upward like a rocket, submerging broad acres with the descent of its boiling flood. Half a mile away, "Old Faithful" spouts every fifty-seven minutes, throwing a stream several feet in diameter to a height of 200 feet. Across the river is the "Bee Hive," whose fountain flies 200 feet in the air, forming a crystal arch beautiful in the sunlight. "The Giantess" has a crater eighteen by fifteen feet in diameter, belching forth such a volume as doubles the amount of water in Fire Hole River, here twenty feet in width and a foot deep. There is a thrill, a groan, a tremor, dense volumes of steam, a rolling and clashing of unseen waves, and a deafening boom as an immense body of water is hurled upward to the sky, its extreme jet reaching 250 feet above the earth.

Next is Gibbon Falls, where, in a wildwood tangle, they drop 150 feet; then Gibbon Cañon, with its sides 2,000 feet high, from which the tourist emerges into Elk Park. In the defile is heard a boom, boom, boom, that never ceases, and from an orifice in the rock comes steam in regular puffs as the pulsation of a great waste pipe of an engine. Monument Geyser and the famous Paint Pots, with their various and vivid hues, are near by. Norris Geyser Basin is the next in order. It is the oldest basin in the park, the hottest and most dangerous for pedestrians. To the right is Mammoth Geyser; when at rest a peep may be had into its gaping throat, and its blood-chilling gurgle can be distinctly heard.

Yellowstone Lake is twenty-five miles from Fire Hole Basin. The altitude of this lake is 7,788 feet. It is thirty miles long and ten to fifteen wide, with numerous islands.

The Natural Bridge of Rock spans Bridge Creek at a height of forty feet and affords carriage room. Down the river twelve miles is Devil's Den; east of this is Mud Volcano. Brimstone Mountain is three miles below. Here pure sulphur is shoveled up by the wagon-load.

The Upper Falls of the Yellowstone are reached by an easy trail. Here the rapids narrow to less than 100 feet, and the overhanging rocks press so closely together that a bridge could be easily thrown across. The water eddies and cascades, and then flies downward 397 feet, while the grandest cañon of the world stretches away 1,500 feet below. The mind cannot grasp that cañon; words cannot paint it; it glows with a life of its own, and with colors of its own, or born of the sun and the spray. Tower Falls and Cañon are twenty miles from this charming spot. Specimen Mountain is forty miles from Fire Hole Basin. It is covered with agate, once wood, stone snakes and fishes, with crystals and petrified roots, while the view from the summit is sublime.

And this is Yellowstone National Park. Words cannot convey a proper realization of its grandeur and magnificence. Nowhere else in America are there such superb views as the park affords; nowhere else such an abundance of finny game; nowhere else such myriads of wild fowl; nowhere else such a delightful camping place or more perfect weather.

This route, with Fire Hole Basin as a centre, brings the tourist near the leading attractions.

From Fire Hole Basin —

The Falls of the Madison are six miles.

Mouth of the Gibbon, ten miles.

Foot of Madison Cañon, eighteen miles.

Falls and Cañon of the Gibbon, thirteen miles.

Monument Geyser, eighteen miles.

Lower Geyser Basin, two miles.

Midway Geyser Basin, five miles.

Upper Geyser Basin, ten miles.

Yellowstone Lake, twenty-five miles.

Yellowstone Falls and Cañon, thirty-five miles.

Remember this route, via the Union Pacific Railway from either Council Bluffs or Kansas City, via Cheyenne, Green River, Granger, and Pocatello, to Beaver Cañon, and thence via stage to Fire Hole Basin.

IDAHO POINTS.

SHOSHONE.

FROM Shoshone Station, which has a population of some 2,000 people, and
fair accommodations for the traveler, there is a branch of the Oregon
Short Line of the Union Pacific Railway running to Bellevue, Hailey,
and Ketchum, the principal towns of the famous Wood River region. It will
pay the tourist to make a digression from the through line to Portland here,
in order to visit this section, which possesses one of the richest silver mines in
the world, and is as yet but little explored. It has a fine climate and plenty of
game.

HAILEY.

Hailey is situated just where Quigley and Croy Gulches unite with the Wood
River Valley, the junction affording a fine view in four directions, embracing
well-cultivated ranches, and ending with the foothills. The climate is mild
and even, and the roads stretching away on all sides are perfect. The mines
at Hailey possess much of interest to the tourist, and a good hotel furnishes
accommodations. The Hot Sulphur Springs here possess unusually good qualities. There are two large swimming-baths, one for ladies and one for gentlemen.
The largest hospital of Alturas County is near. A two-mile drive from Hailey
takes the tourist to the beautiful valley of Croy Gulch, with an altitude of about
5,300 feet. The Bolton Hot Springs, five miles from Hailey, are also very
efficacious in relieving and curing rheumatism. Bellevue, just north of Hailey,
is a pretty little town.

KETCHUM.

Ketchum, a rapidly growing town of about 2,000 to 3,000 people, lies just
beyond Bellevue, and is beautifully situated at the head of the Wood River
Valley. At this point, Wood River is as clear as crystal, and rich in the finest

of mountain trout. The vicinity surrounding affords good hunting, and elk and bear abound. The mines round about Ketchum are large, and will well repay inspection. The Guyer Hot Springs, two miles by stage from Ketchum, are noted for their medicinal waters, and are of high repute throughout the neighboring country. There are many objects of interest, both for the tourist and pleasure seeker, in and about Ketchum. The scenery is beautiful, and the climate all that could be desired.

BOISE CITY.

From Shoshone Station, passing westward, the next town of importance is Boise City, which is now reached from Nampa on the Oregon Short Line of the Union Pacific Railway, via the Idaho Central. Boise City is nineteen miles from Nampa, and has an elevation of about 2,800 feet. It has a population of about 6,000, has good hotel accomodations, and is a point of interest to the tourist. Boise City is the largest, wealthiest, and most attractive town in the Territory, with good schools and pleasant homes. It is in the centre of the Idaho fruit belt. A great many medicinal springs are to be found within the immediate neighborhood of Boise City, easy of access, and possessing many charms both of water and scenery.

GUYER HOT SPRINGS.

This romantic little mountain resort is situated about two miles from the town of Ketchum, Idaho, on the Wood River branch of the Oregon Short Line, sixty-nine miles from Shoshone. Regular hacks run to and from the springs, in connection with the branch trains. The springs are comparatively unknown outside of Idaho, but are destined to become famous for the well-known medicinal qualities of the waters and the great natural beauty of the place. The springs, about fifteen in number, gush out from the mountain side intensely hot, and are conveyed a short distance by pipe to the bathhouse, where there are two large plunge baths and quite a number of single rooms with tubs. The waters are good for all nervous complaints, rheumatism, skin and blood affections. This place is much resorted to by tourists and invalids. It is a beautiful, quiet mountain retreat. The accommodations for guests are first class, and in addition to the hotel, there are bathhouses, bowling-alleys, croquet and tennis grounds, swings, band-stands and dancing-platforms—everything, in short, to make a visit pleasant.

SODA SPRINGS.

The Soda Springs are located on the main line of the Oregon Short Line branch of the Union Pacific Railway and are within a stone's throw of the railway station bearing the same name. They are in Bingham County, Idaho, sixty miles east of Pocatello, in the depression of the Wasatch Mountains. Their altitude is 5,779 feet above sea-level, with snowy mountains perpetually in sight. Ages ago the Indians sought these springs because they discovered that the waters were a sovereign remedy for many of their ills, and that something about the air and the water gave them, at least in part, what Ponce de Leon dreamed of finding, a fountain of water which had within it the elements to insure to those who drank the boon of eternal youth. So through the centuries the Indians held their treasure, until civilization claimed them for her own.

The waters of these springs are charged with bicarbonate of soda, bicarbonate of potash, chloride of sodium and potash, sulphate of magnesia, bicarbonate of magnesia, lime, alumina, silica, carbonate of iron, free carbonic acid gas, and a multitude of other ingredients. They are a specific for the cure of all manner of indigestion, kidney troubles, even up to advanced symptoms of Bright's disease, and diabetes, dropsy, and a thousand kindred ills.

Of the tens of millions who inhabit the United States east of the Rocky Mountains, probably not one in a thousand has ever heard of Soda Springs, Idaho. Probably not one in ten thousand has any idea of their rare medicinal properties, and not one in a hundred thousand realizes that in comparison with them all the famous spas of the Old World sink into insignificance. They take away all appetite for spirituous liquors, and the water is the most pleasant for table use that has ever been found.

Frémont's account of the excellence of these springs will be found in his official reports. In 1850, Mormon explorers traversing the country reported the marvels of the springs, and later on, the chiefs of the Mormon Church visited the place, and Brigham Young solemnly blessed them.

But, despite the virtues of the water, backed by the blessing of Brigham Young. Soda Springs remained an out-of-the-way place, little frequented and little known, until the Union Pacific Railway built the Oregon Short Line, from Green River and Granger, on the main line, to Portland, Oregon, which line runs directly by the springs, where now Pullman palace cars land passengers from all portions of the country. These springs are within fifty hours' ride of Council Bluffs or Kansas City. One of the chief inducements which decided the company to build the line was to open these springs to the public. Last year the Soda Springs Company was organized and began bottling the water, which, by a secret process, retains all its pleasant and medicinal properties; and this water is now on sale throughout the East and West.

The climate of the springs is as wonderful as the water. The topography of the country is interesting; the springs cover a large area, and those who desire to, can spend the summer there camping out. The water, the air, and the sky are free, and their virtues, like those of the Master, go out to all who are able to touch so much as the hem of their robes. The days in the summer are warm, while the nights are invariably cool enough for blankets. The surrounding country abounds in fine hunting, while Blackfoot Creek, ten miles away, reached by a natural road, supplies the best trout fishing in the West. These springs are readily reached from the east and west by the Oregon Short Line branch of the Union Pacific Railway, and from the north and south by the Utah & Northwestern branch of the Union Pacific Railway, and they will soon be recognized as one of the most wonderful sanitariums in the world. Good accommodations can be had at the Idanha Hotel, which is run by the Pacific Hotel Company. Tourists and health and pleasure seekers will be amply repaid by a visit to these wonderful springs.

THE GREAT SHOSHONE FALLS OF THE SNAKE RIVER.

These falls are readily reached by a stage ride of twenty-five miles from Shoshone Station, on the Oregon Short Line branch of the Union Pacific Railway. The tourist takes this ride in a genuine Concord stage, pulled by four horses, presided over by one of those thoroughly western characters, a Rocky Mountain stage driver. He is generally tall and angular, sunburnt and jovial, full of stories and border vernacular. The road is good and across a desert that is no pretense. No streams or springs gladden its barren surface, broken only by grassless knolls and blocks of lava, over which the horses fairly fly, the downward impulse of one hill carrying them up the next. The question is often asked, where all of the lava over which the stage rolls comes from, as there are no volcanic mountains for hundreds of miles. The whole area was once a simmering mass, that, being submerged, resulted in many curious fractures, into some of which an article dropped will go clinking from side to side until the noise dies away, apparently without bottom being reached. It is in such a crevice that the Lost River disappears never to be seen again. The Snake River is indicated by no sign, when all at once from the edge of a vast chasm, smooth between stupendous walls, it is seen flowing hundreds of feet below. What power has wrought this sculpture? It does not seem possible that water, even in untold ages, could work into the lava and granite, leaving the pillared heights to testify to its work. The roar of the falls is heard, and, picking its way down the slope, the four-in-hand pauses within earshot of the solemn music, and the baptism of the spray. Having arrived in the evening, it is well to rest in a luxurious bed and await the revelation of sunlight. It comes like a gleam of intelligence, passing over the mighty cañon. The walls, rising hundreds of feet, catch the glint before it reaches the bottom of the gorge and the river, and from height to height the beams of the morning flash signals. There are no mountains by which to judge altitude, but a drop out of the world seems to be taken. The overwhelming massiveness of the gorge baffles all eye-measure of the stupendous rift, out of which a climb would be impossible. The close-pressing lava towers are as sombre as a prison-house. After breakfast a boat is found in the little willow-fringed bayou and launched upon the open river—which here broadens to a lake—but silent, stern, and powerful the current sweeps along. That cloud of steam ahead rises from Shoshone Falls, and that ceaseless clamor is the great voice of its waters. There is an easy trail upon landing, which leads through a border of fir, and a rest is taken upon Point Lookout. Just then the sun breaks forth in renewed radiance, and from cliff to cliff there springs a bow as perfect as was ever made glorious in the heavens—an arc of beauteous coloring against a background of glittering, beadlike foam tumbling in crystal chaos 220 feet, the circling halo losing its bases in the turmoil and the mist, with an unbroken crescent above. The rock foothold quivers, a gentle bath dews the uncovered head, while the spirit soars as lofty as the illumined spray. There is a spell like that of a nameless melody in the awfulness of the irresistible plunge. Niagara is different, but not superior. Where Niagara is calm, Shoshone is tempestuous ; where Niagara pours over evenly, Shoshone bursts into a million wild jets, each with a diamond's lustre ; where Niagara is environed by common-place landscapes, Shoshone dashes from between rocks nearly a thousand feet high, stately and time-stained, and its surroundings are weird and supernatural. Seven distinct channels are to be seen forming a number of brilliant falls, before finally there is a grand reunion of the waters, and so united, over they go, to be lost in the rage of a terrible surge, to riot in an infuriate whirlpool, and to rise soft as the feather of a bird and be touched by the sun to splendor.

Only a stone's throw from the shore, Eagle Rock has never been touched by man, but on the top-most crest an eagle hovers with wrathful mien over her young. Standing face toward the falls, on the extreme left is Pulpit Rock ; next, Prospect Point. Cedar, Walgamotts, and Bells are a chain of islands across, the divided flow of the Snake coming between them. Prospect Point and Pulpit Rock overlook Bridal Veil, one of the brightest of the smaller falls. The former is immediately in front of the site selected for the large hotel. Lover's Leap affords one of the finest views. Facing it are the lesser falls and the unbroken front of the great one—750 feet from shore to shore—unbroken because no rocks mar its contour, and yet broken, for it is not a glassy sheet of water that makes the leap ending in glistening foaming spray. Looking aghast you cling to the withered pine marking the spot where the lovers fell 750 feet in front of the maddened, malignant torrent, devilish in the delight it takes in sweeping with a rush which nothing but the eternal rocks could withstand, torn and tossed into billions of sparkling threads with a constant play of prismatic hues changing quicker than thought, half enveloped in its own mist, and then the wind carrying that away, leaving it unobscured, in sublimity unmatched and indescribable. A long, winding trail leads past the Natural Bridge and the Devil's Flues, the last apertures reaching down to the level of the stream below the falls. Their origin is a mystery. The trail is half hidden in luxuriant shrubbery, the shallow soil being constantly drenched with spray. It is no place for the lame, halt, or blind. Each eye must be open, each hand and foot alert for a hold. The scramble is for 850 feet. From below, there is such a change from the point of inspection, that the treat is entirely new. Here the opposite wall, black and frowning, is over a thousand feet sheer. A thousand feet means more in such a place than two thousand among the mountains. The vaulted dome is near by. It is made by the throwing together of huge rocks. It is a conical chamber 175 feet in height, and with an atmosphere cooling as a draught from the fountain. From the top there is a steady sprinkle of water—a shower-bath which, falling year after year, has worn a hollow known as Diana s Bath. Surely a goddess could covet no place more charming. The water fills this to overflowing. It is nearly ice cold. Drink it freely. It is nectar. The sides of the chamber are wet and green with moss. High out of reach are brilliant festoons of flowers, growing from the rock. It is an ideal place to lunch, and in itself a wonder.

It is now time to go back, re-cross the river, or row up to Twin Falls. The two sets of falls are three miles apart. A portion of the way a boat may be used, and a trail completes the journey. There is some good, honest perspiration attendant upon the row to Clark's Point, beyond the Devil's Corral. The latter is an inclosure with only one entrance. Clark's Point is a huge fortress jutting into the stream. It is a curious place to be, in that long defile, and it is not designed for a thoroughfare. The ride seems short, but the walk does not. An acute ear detects a suppressed roar coming jointly from above and below. The waves of sound from Great Shoshone, and from the Upper Falls meet and mingle somewhere in the gorge. Finally the falls are reached, and standing above them is recompense enough for all the toil. The view along the cañon in itself is worth a journey of miles. There is a frightful snakiness about the river, an appalling strength as it enters the rapids, and a glorying in this strength as it leaps below. The stream is divided by a tower of solid rock into two channels, across which an easy toss would carry a stone. All that mass of water, which three miles farther is so magnificent with its frontage of 750 feet, is here condensed into these narrow spaces, descending through them 180 feet, so that even these falls, secondary though they be to Great Shoshone Falls, are higher than the famed Niagara. A constant vapor arises from them, and when the air is still, bedews the rocks far higher than the upper level. Yet, for all its great height, it is the superior height of the rocks which makes the greatest impression. At the crest of the walls there is no grade to correspond with the sinking of the river, so that the chasm gets deeper and deeper until beyond the Great Shoshone Falls it is stupendous.

The float down the river is something to be always remembered. To sit and calmly glide, to dip in the cool stream and drink, to watch the serried columns of lava glide by, and listen to the song of the eddies, is a pleasure. Night is coming on, and the shadows begin to stretch darkly across. The gloom makes the rocks look more weird and supernatural, and the motion and the twilight belong to the realm of the mystic. The cañon is a wonderful whispering gallery. A whistle awakes a thousand echoes, and to a shout each castle perched above gives back a loud response. The notes of a cornet are taken up and repeated fainter and more faint till they die away in melody. And so challenging the rocks to reply to a tune, and every challenge being accepted and hurled back with treble force, the notes are again repeated far away, long after the air is finished.

After supper a walk is taken to Prospect Point, and, as if in greeting, just then the mist changes from its billowy white to a rainbow mass, which the lunar rays make softly brilliant, and which seem to fade away in farewell as the moon is lost under shifting clouds.

No one can inspect this place thoroughly in a day. The day is simply a hint. The Great Shoshone Falls demand a day, the Upper Falls another, and the cañon still another.

As yet the surroundings of the falls are as wild and untouched as when the pilgrims for Astoria, wandering through the wilderness years ago, marveled at their great beauty. And such is the Great Shoshone Falls, one of the greatest points of interest in the world.

POCATELLO.

This town is on the Oregon Short Line branch of the Union Pacific Railway, at the junction with the Utah & Northern branch, 153 miles from Ogden, Utah, and 245 miles from Green River. Its elevation is 4,466 feet above sea-level. The Utah & Northern Railroad stretches off north to Beaver Cañon (where stage connection for the Yellowstone National Park is made), Butte, Garrison, and Helena, and to Ogden, Salt Lake City, and Garfield Beach, on the shores of Great Salt Lake. Pocatello is a lively little town of some 2,000 people, and growing rapidly. Here the division headquarters and machine shops of the railway are located. The climate is cool and bracing, and the scenery around it superb. The country is broken and rugged, but there are pleasant, fertile valleys, and the Fort Hall Indian Reservation, in which Pocatello is situated, is a beautiful stretch of country.

MONTANA POINTS.

L EAVING Green River and Granger, on the main line of the Union
Pacific, through Soda Springs and Pocatello, via the Oregon Short Line
branch of the Union Pacific Railway, and thence from Pocatello north
on the Utah & Northern Railroad, and passing the Three Tetons and Beaver
Cañon, where connection by stage line is made for the Yellowstone National
Park, a few miles bring the tourist within the confines of Montana. Passing
the water line, Red Rock Station is the first point of interest. Here the
scenery is wild, and there is a peculiar formation of points of jagged land, the
highest of which is Red Rock, which juts up some 500 feet, and may be seen
in either direction for twenty miles. Then through Dillon, which is in Beaver
Head Valley, and one of the thriving towns of Montana, Silver Bow is reached.
From Silver Bow the Montana Union Railroad, an auxilliary line of the Union
Pacific Railway, branches off, one spur running to Butte City, another through
Stuart to Garrison, where connection is made for Helena, and still another
from Stuart to Anaconda.

BUTTE CITY.

Butte City, with an elevation of 5,492 feet above sea-level, is the largest
mining camp in the world, not even excepting Leadville, Colorado. Standing
next to the Lake Superior regions in the production of copper, and first of all
in silver output, attention has been drawn to it from all over the world. Butte
has a population of some 25,000 people, is the possessor of fine hotels and all
the modern conveniences of a large city. It is the greatest silver producer, not
alone of Montana, but of the Rocky Mountain mineral belt. It is situated on
a gentle slope and is surrounded by rugged and beautiful scenery, and takes its
name from the point known as the Big Butte, located just north of the original
town. It is ten miles to the main range of the Rockies, but towering foothills

(43)

have formed the basin where Butte flourishes. From Butte City, points of interest in Silver Bow, Jefferson, and Madison Counties can be readily reached. Butte is a healthy place, and blessed with a pure and bracing atmosphere. Butte City presents many attractions to the tourist and health and pleasure seeker.

ANACONDA.

From Stuart, the Montana Union also has a branch to Anaconda. Here is located the largest smelting works in the world, the consumption of coal alone for these works being 300 tons per day, and the yield from copper ore is enormous. From Stuart, the pretty little town of Deer Lodge is but a short distance, and is a point of much interest.

GARRISON.

Further on is Garrison, a place of note, being the junction of the Montana Union branch of the Union Pacific Railway with the Northern Pacific, and formerly the transfer point of passengers going to Portland. But since the opening of the Oregon Short Line, the Route is via Huntington, which is the direct line to Portland ; the Garrison Route is used for Helena business.

HELENA.

Helena is the capital of Montana, with an elevation of 4,266 feet above the sea-level, and a population of about 20,000. Helena is also a mining camp, and is reached over the Union Pacific Railway, via Garrison, and the Northern Pacific Railroad. It is beautifully situated; Fort Benton to the north, Bozeman to the east, Virginia City to the south, with Butte City and Deer Lodge to the west. It has fine hotels, clubs, banks, newspapers, street cars—in fact everything that contributes to city life. There are many attractions for the tourist. Mount Helena is to be climbed, and the view from its summit well repays the labor. There are pleasant drives, one of the most popular leading to Hot Springs, four miles away. Prickly Pear Cañon presents attractive features. "The Gate of the Mountains," where the Missouri River bursts through, infinitely surpasses the Hudson Highlands, and for 100 miles down stream there is a succession of pillared hills, of castles, of eroded stone, of caves, and of falls. East of Helena are the White Sulphur Springs, Hell Gate Cañon, and the Devil's Watch Tower. Northwest is Flat Lake, twenty-eight by ten miles, and the Twin Cascades, Elizabeth and Alice, falling 2,000 feet.

OREGON POINTS.

O REGON has nothing to lose by a close inspection of what she has to offer in the way of climate, productions, scenery, and pleasure resorts. Within its immense area of 96,000 square miles all that is desirable in the make up of a great and prosperous State is to be found, and its wonderful resources augur well for its future.

From Nampa, Idaho, the Oregon Short Line, passing through the towns of Caldwell, Payette, Ontario, and Weiser, skirts along the boundary line of Idaho and Oregon, following the Snake River, which it crosses and re-crosses, first in Idaho, then in Oregon, until Huntington, just within Oregon, is reached, where it starts directly across the State. Huntington is the junction of the Oregon Short Line with the Oregon Railway & Navigation Company, an auxiliary line of the Union Pacific Railway. Baker City, Union, and La Grande, important towns beyond Huntington, are passed. Just beyond La Grande, in the Grande Ronde Valley, comes a passage in the Blue Mountains, replete with the dark beauty of the pine and the rippling brook and waterfall.

THE GRANDE RONDE VALLEY.

The Grande Ronde Valley presents many points of interest to the tourist, and a sojourn here will amply repay the visitor. It is one of the most fertile valleys of the Pacific slope. The Grande Ronde River flows in from the Blue Mountains, and follows an extremely crooked channel through the valley. Fish and game abound. Mountain streams and copious springs break forth on every hand, converting portions of the valley into a beautiful meadow.

Leaving La Grande, and passing over the summit at Meacham, on through the Umatilla Reservation to Pendleton, and over the Cascade Mountains, the tourist reaches "The Dalles" Station, on the Columbia River, the commencement of the "The Dalles" of the Columbia.

"THE DALLES" OF THE COLUMBIA.

All along, the sights have been absorbing in their varied aspects; but it is only when a pause is made at "The Dalles" Station that the true grandeur of the scenery of the Columbia River is impressed upon the mind. There are good accommodations here, and from this point the noble river, surging and whirling to the sea, breaking the image rocks into wave fragments, occupies the mind of the beholder. The Columbia is one of the world's great rivers, affording a waterway that is navigable for traffic for over 200 miles. Upon it, near its mouth, the largest ocean steamers ply with safety. It is Oregon's artery, throbbing with trade. Its largest tributary is the Willamette, draining the valley of the same name, and being navigable for vessels of any size to Portland. There can be nothing more inspiring than the ride along "The Dalles" of the Columbia, with the shining river on one side and the towering battlements of the shore on the other. The scene is one of continued magnificence. The grottos, in which are moss-garlanded cascades, almost hidden under the dense foliage, are most inviting and beautiful. Multnomah Falls and their surroundings are a bit of fairy land. There are scores of smaller falls—mere ribbons some of them—but all clear and dashing, and banked by a wealth of moss. The lofty summits over which they pour are reproduced in the river, and made doubly impressive. For miles upon miles this wild scenery continues, and a thousand times the tourist thinks the climax has been reached, only to acknowledge later that something grander has developed, particularly when Cape Horn, 700 feet sheer height, Castle Rock, 1,000 feet, Gibraltar, and Hallet's Hades burst into view. Along the line of the Rhine, or the Rhone, or the Hudson, there is nothing that will compare with the stately palisades of the Columbia, with their cool recesses, kept sunless by the overhanging rocks, and watered by the melting snows of their own summits. A splendid view can be had of Mt. Hood, Mt. St. Helen's, and the Cascades, where the scenery surpasses anything of the kind in the world. From Hood River Station the traveler will find good stages to convey him over an excellent road to the base of Mt. Hood, twenty-five miles distant. The view from Mt. Hood is simply incomparable, and the trip from Hood River Station to Mt. Hood is made through some of the most extraordinary scenery in the world.

Mr. E. McD. Johnstone speaks of Mt. Hood as follows : " The view from the summit of Hood is one of unsurpassed grandeur, and probably includes in its range a greater number of high peaks and vast mountain chains, grand forests and mighty rivers than any other mountain in North America. Looking across the Columbia, the ghostly pyramids of Adams and St. Helen, with their connecting ridges of eternal snow, first catch the eye ; then comes the silent, lofty Ranier, with the blue waters of Puget Sound and the rugged Olympian Mountains for a background; and away to the extreme north (nearly to

H. B. M.'s dominions), veiled in earth mists and scarcely discernible from the towering cumuli that inswathe it, lies Mt. Baker. Looking south over Oregon the view embraces the Three Sisters (all at one time), Jefferson, Diamond Peak, Scott, Pitt, and if it be a favorable day, and you have a good glass, you may see Shasta, 250 miles away. The westward view is down over the lower coast range, the Umpqua, Calapooya, and Rogue River Mountains, with their sunny, upland valleys, and away out over the restless sea. In the opposite direction, across the illimitable plains of Eastern Oregon, to the Azure Blue Mountains; down, almost to the foot of this mountain, 'rolls the Columbia,' through the narrow, rugged gorge of 'The Dalles,' 250 miles of its winding course being visible. The entire length of the great Willamette Valley, with its pleasant, prosperous towns and gently flowing river, its broad, fertile farms, like rich mosaics, with borders of dark-green woodlands, is spread out in great beauty under the western slope of Mt. Hood."

PORTLAND.

From "The Dalles" Station, the trip to Portland can be made either via water or rail, the Oregon Railway & Navigation Company having a line of fine boats that make the trip by water.

Arrived at Portland, the metropolis of Oregon, which needs no mention here, the tourist can reach other important points in Oregon, and that not far off country, Alaska, an extraordinary and almost unknown domain. To the tourist, Alaska presents many points of interest. Its curious people, wonderful scenery, extinct volcanoes, magnificent glaciers, hot springs, sulphur lakes, and boiling marshes, well repay the tourist for making the trip. The verdure, flowers, and birds of this Northland dispel the popular illusion of its frigid temperature. A trip to Alaska will be something to think of in after years.

From Portland to San Francisco, the trip can be made in the iron steamships of the Oregon Railway & Navigation Company, which favorably compare with the best ocean steamers on the Atlantic for safety, speed, and comfort; or by rail over the Mt. Shasta route of the Central Pacific Railroad (or the Southern Pacific Company). After the long ride by rail, the ocean voyage makes a pleasing break, the murmur of the ocean breezes, and the rythmic cadence of the waves as they kiss the sides of the noble ship form a fitting finale to the overland trip across the continent.

CRATER LAKE.

Crater Lake, Oregon, can be reached from Medford, Oregon, on the Mt. Shasta Route of the Southern Pacific Company, and Stage Line to Fort Klamath, the military post in the Klamath Indian Reservation. The distance by stage from Medford to Fort Klamath is about 100 miles and, from Fort Klamath to the Crater Lake about twenty-five miles.

Crater Lake is situated in the Oregon National Park, about twenty-five miles north of Ft. Klamath, among the summits of the Cascade Range. It is the crater of a long extinct volcano, and its waters, formerly believed to be fathomless, were found by the measurements of the geological survey to be 4,000 feet deep.

The surface of the lake is 6,351 feet above the level of the sea, and its shores rise almost perpendicularly from the water's edge to a height of from 1,000 to over 2,000 feet—that is, to an elevation of from 7,351 feet to over 8,351 feet above sea-level; three-fourths the height of Mt. Hood, only 1,000 feet lower than Mt. St. Helens, and 2,000 feet above Mt. Washington.

It is oblong in shape, being seven miles long and six miles broad, and covering an area of about forty-two square miles. Out of its abysmal depths rise numerous islands, towering precipitously to enormous heights. Shag Rock is 2,115 feet high, Dutton Cliff, 2,109 feet, Llao Rock, 2,000 feet, Heliotrope Station, 1,965 feet, and Wizard Island towers 845 feet above the surface of the water.

It is in many respects the most wonderful body of water in the world. Lake Baikal, in Siberia, is eighty feet deeper, but it is a sea in comparison, covering a space of fifty-four by 397 miles.

Though it lies on the very ridge of the great Cascade Range, and Mt. Scott, close by, towers in snowy majesty to a height of 9,117 feet above the sea, the ascent is easy, and wagons can be driven to its very brink. The visitor approaching the spot, suddenly emerges from the belt of encircling timber into an amphitheatre of desolation. Huge masses of rocks, lava, cinders, scoria, and pumice stone, lie scattered and piled all around ; rocky pinnacles tower skyward on every hand ; and just beyond rises a semi-circle of mountain peaks, from 200 to 1,000 feet high. Advancing a few steps farther, one is suddenly, without warning, on the brink of the abyss, and cautiously peering over its edge, the inky waters of the lake are seen in glassy calm, or in stormy tumult, 2,000 feet below in the very bowels of the mountain. The dizzy walls are scarred, melted, and blackened from the belching floods of flame and molten lava that ages since were vomited up from the Plutonian furnaces of the central earth ; and lying flat upon the ground, a stone dropped will almost pass from sight before it strikes a projection in the perpendicular wall.

It is a sublime, a majestic, an awful—almost a horrible spectacle, and the head swims with the contemplation of it. It is little wonder that the simple-minded natives believe it to be inhabited by ilaos, or devils, and regard a curious glance therein as a profanation. Their traditions teach them that ages ago it was the scene of terrible convulsions—of fiery struggles between warring spirits, and that the conquerors retain possession to this day. Geologists confirm these traditions, in teaching us that the mountain once rose to a height of 10,000 to 20,000 feet, and was a peculiarly active volcano, the peak having been gradually eroded by the violence of the successive eruptions to its present height.

The vent of the final eruption was Wizard Island, a regularly conical mountain of cinder, with a cup-shaped top, usually filled with snow.

There are several descents by which access can be had to the level of the lake, where the visitor may enjoy the strange luxury of a boat ride over the waters of Jules Verne's "Central Sea," and look up, as it were, through the chimney of the globe, and picture the terrible energies that once found through it a vent, with fire, and smoke, and quakings, and vast thunders of torment, compared to which the throes of Ætna are but pigmy tremors.

THE MOUNT SHASTA ROUTE.

(FROM PORTLAND TO SAN FRANCISCO.)

The Mt. Shasta route is very interesting, and the tourist should see its marvels to fully appreciate the wonders of Oregon and California. This route, through the western portion of Oregon, southward through the northern portion of California, from Portland to San Francisco, passes through a country fertile in resources, and rich in points of scenic interest. Particularly is this true of Northern California, which will in time equal and excel the southern portions of the State in wealth and population, and the rapid strides this section has been making since the completion of the Mount Shasta route by the Southern Pacific Company augurs well for its future importance and prosperity.

The Mt. Shasta route takes its name from Mt. Shasta, which is situated on its line in California. It is one of the most wonderful mountains in the world, as well as one of the largest. It has a number of peaks; Main Peak, altitude, 14,440; Thumb Rock, 13,000, and Crater Peak, 12,900. The view from the different portions of the mountain is incomparably lovely, and cannot be excelled on the American continent. Other points of interest are Mt. Hood (which is reached by stage from this line of road), Umpqua and Rogue River Mountains. The Rogue River Valley, the Siskyous, Strawberry Valley, one of the scenic wonders of the Pacific coast, the plains of Northern California, Upper Soda Springs in Sacramento Cañon, Lower Soda Springs, the Sacramento River, which rises at the base of Mt. Shasta, and is one of the most beautiful rivers in the world, and Mossbrae Falls, are a few of the wonders presented to the tourist in the trip from Portland to San Francisco, via the Mt. Shasta route.

UTAH POINTS.

OGDEN.

OGDEN is one of the western termini of the Union Pacific Railway. It has an elevation of about 4,294 feet above the sea-level. It has a population of about 12,000 people, and is steadily gaining all the time. While its growth has been slow, it has been on a solid basis. The enormous supplies in shipments from the great country tributary to it give employment in their transfer to a large number of men. Here are located the division headquarters and shops of the Union Pacific Railway and the Central Pacific Railroad. It has good schools, hotels, banks, and churches, and the surrounding country possesses much to attract the tourist.

Just north of Ogden, and beyond the Utah Hot Springs, is the celebrated Cache Valley, oval in form, and surrounded by mountains and trimmed with green-fringed brooks and rivulets. Through this valley runs the Utah & Northern branch to Pocatello, and north of the valley is the famous Port Neuf Cañon, unusually picturesque in formation.

OGDEN CAÑON.

Ogden Cañon, one of Utah's chief scenic attractions, is reached by a half hour's drive over a good road from Ogden. The Ogden River, which courses between its walls, is a famous trout stream. The sides of this cañon are very precipitous and picturesque, rivaling the American Fork in the variety and character of their striking features. At the head of the cañon is an elevated park, called Ogden Park, and beyond this the drive may be extended to Cache and Bear Lake Valleys.

UTAH HOT SPRINGS.

These springs are sometimes called Red Springs, and sometimes Ogden Springs. They are just nine miles north of Ogden, and are readily reached from there over the Utah & Northern branch of the Union Pacific Railway to

Hot Springs Station, which is a regular station on the road, and the springs are but a few steps away. All trains stop at the door of the hotel. This hotel is plainly, but comfortably furnished, accommodating about 150 people, and additional accommodations are being provided every season. These springs have an elevation of some 4,500 feet above sea-level, and are far superior to the celebrated Hot Springs of Arkansas. The main spring boils up at the foot of a low ridge of the Wasatch Mountains, a short distance east of the railway station. These springs impart a red hue to the surrounding soil. Their temperature is so high that the hand cannot be held in the water without great pain. The water is conducted into the hotel from the springs in wooden pipes for private bathing and for the great open bath, when it becomes cool enough for use. These springs are patronized all the year around, and are very efficacious in curing rheumatism, neuralgia, catarrh, and all skin, blood, and kidney diseases. The waters are intensely hot, and their chief constituents are iron, magnesia, soda, and salt.

The bracing air of the Wasatch Range, mingling with the saline breezes of the Great Salt Lake, with the pure water of these thermal, balsamic springs, nowhere excelled for drinking or bathing purposes, produce a natural combination of marvelously curative properties.

The flow is about 156,000 gallons of water every twenty-four hours, at a temperature of 131 Fahrenheit. A close analysis of the water by Prof. Spencer F. Baird, of the Smithsonian Institution, Washington, D. C., shows that besides containing carbonate of iron in heavy deposits, it also contains:

	Grains to the gallon.
Silica	2.687
Alumina	0.234
Calcium sulphate	18.074
Calcium chloride	170.498
Potassium chloride	97.741
Sodium chloride	1,052.475
Magnesium chloride	1.067
Magnesium carbonate	11.776

The bathing accommodations consist of a number of private tubs, for vapor or steam and hot mud baths. The latter is the great Indian cure for rheumatism. Besides supplying these baths, this wonderful water is run into an outside summer bath 166 x 204 feet, three feet deep at the upper and seven at the lower side, arranged with foot runs and spring boards, thus affording amusement for hundreds at a time.

GARFIELD BEACH AND GREAT SALT LAKE.

Garfield Beach, or Black Rock, is eighteen miles from Salt Lake City, on the shores of the Great Salt Lake, and is reached from Salt Lake City by the Utah & Nevada branch of the Union Pacific Railway. During the season trains run back and forth at frequent intervals during the day and evening. It is the only real sand beach on the lake, and is considered by many to be the finest in the world. It should be and will be the great resort of the continent. It is not a sullen, listless sheet of water, beating idly on the shores, barren and repellant; but on the contrary it is as beautiful a sheet of water as can be found anywhere. The waves are a bright blue or green, and as they dance on its surface it would be hard to tell which color prevails. The water supports no life. Its constant sinking and rising is only one of its many curious phases. The sensation upon entering the water is novel and congenial. In the long sunny days of June, July, August, and September the water becomes delightfully warm, much warmer than the ocean. It is 21 per cent. salt, while the ocean is only 3 per cent. The water is so dense that a person is sustained on its surface indefinitely without effort. Experience has proven its great hygienic effects. Owing to the stimulating effect of the brine upon the skin, or the saline air upon the lungs, or both together, the appetite is stimulated, and after a bath bathers are ready for a hearty meal. The baths are extremely invigorating. If there is any abrasion upon the skin it will smart for an instant when it touches the brine, but after the bath the smarting is gone never to return, and after rinsing off in the fresh water, provided in every bathroom, there is a sense of cleanliness more perfect than any other bath can produce. A fine bathhouse accommodating 400 people has been erected at Garfield Beach, in connection with which there is a first-class restaurant, and a large dancing pavilion built out into the lake, all of which are run by the Pacific Hotel Company, under the supervision of the Union Pacific Railway. At the restaurant excellent meals can be had during the entire season. The buildings at Garfield Beach are modern, have every convenience, and were erected last year at a great cost. It is proposed to erect a large hotel on the beach, although the ready access which is had to and from the Salt Lake City hotels, has heretofore rendered a hotel at Garfield Beach unnecessary. The view from the pavilion at Garfield Beach is one of surpassing loveliness. The mountains on the shore form a fine background to the rippling waters of the lake, which stretch out on either hand before the beholder, dancing in the sunlight, sometimes a beautiful blue, and at other times green, with three or four of the largest islands in full view, which, in the distance, have a peculiar purplish hue.

When Great Salt Lake was discovered it was out of the world, but it is now isolated no longer. Every one taking the transcontinental trip on the Union Pacific Railway is afforded a detour free of charge to Salt Lake City, and once in Salt Lake City, the great lake must be seen, and this lake, as a special feature, is becoming better and better known every year. It is called the "Dead Sea of America."

The first mention of Great Salt Lake was made by the Baron La Hontan in 1689, who gathered some vague knowledge of its existence from the western Indians. Captain Bonneville sent a party from Green River in 1833 to make its

circuit, but they gave it up on striking the desert on the northwest, lost their
way, and finally wandered into California. Until Colonel Frémont visited it in
1842, on his way to Oregon, it is probable that its dead waters had never been
invaded, or the solemn stillness of its islands broken by the pale face, although
mention is made of the "Great Salt Sea" in the writings of other explorers.
Brigham Young and the Mormon pioneers in '47, were the first setlers along
its shores. From this time this region ceased to be a terra incognita.

There have been many analyses made of the waters of the Great Salt Lake,
all of them agreeing that it is a solution consisting of chloride of sodium or
common salt, or sulphates of silver, potash, alum, and the chloride of magne-
sium. The following comparison of solid contents and specific gravity may be
of interest:

	Solid Contents. Per Cent.	Specific Gravity.
Great Salt Lake water	13.8	1.107
Dead Sea water	21.0	1.116
Ocean water	3.5	1.026

One of the most recent reliable analyses of the waters of the Great
Salt Lake, by Prof. O. D. Allern, of New Haven, Conn., gave the following
results:

	Solids. Per Cent.
Chloride of sodium	79.11
Chloride of magnesia	9.95
Sulphate of soda	6.22
Sulphate of potassa	3.58
Sulphate of lime	0.57
Excess of chlorine	0.57
Total	100.00

The Jordan carries into the Great Salt Lake ten grains of salt per gallon of
water. Great Salt Lake has no outlet, and its fluctuating level is determined
by the balance between in-flowing springs and solar evaporation. On the surrounding mountains are water lines rising in steps to a thousand feet above its
surface, showing that in ancient times a great body of water occupied its basin.
This ancient body, which was known as Lake Bonneville, was 345 miles long
from north to south, and 135 miles broad, and its vestiges are on so grand
a scale that they have attracted the attention of not only geologists, but of
every observant traveler. The principal islands are Antelope and Stansbury,
on which are rocky ridges ranging north and south, and rising abruptly from
the lake to an altitude of 3,000 feet. The view from the summit of Antelope is
grand and magnificent, embracing the whole lake, the islands and the encircling
mountains, covered with snow—a superb picture set in a frame-work of silver.
The scenery on the eastern side of Stansbury is fine. Peak towers above peak,
and cliff beyond cliff in lofty magnificence, while, crowning the summit, the
dome frowns in gloomy solitude upon the varied scene of bright waters,

scattered verdure, and boundless plains of the western shore, in the arid desolation below. Descending one way from the dome, a gorge, at first almost shut up between perpendicular cliffs of white sandstone, opens out into a superb, wide and gently sloping valley, sheltered on each side to the very water's edge by cliffs, effectually protected from all winds except on the east, and covered with the most luxuriant growth of bunch grass. Of the minor islands there are Fremont, Carrington, Gunnison, Dolphin, Mud, Egg. Hat, and several islands without a name.

Great Salt Lake covers an area of 2,500 square miles, and its surface is higher than the average height of the Alleghany Mountains. Its mean depth propably does not exceed twenty feet, while the deepest place, between Antelope and Stansbury Islands, is sixty feet. The water is of a beautiful aqua-marine hue, and so clear that the bottom can be seen to the depth of four fathoms. Great Salt Lake is one of the greatest curiosities of America. Its extreme dimensions are about eighty miles in length by about fifty miles in width, and its elevation about 4,000 feet. ·Great Salt Lake is a wonderful place, and to be appreciated must be seen.

SALT LAKE CITY.

Salt Lake City is reached from Ogden via the Utah Central branch of the Union Pacific Railway, thirty-seven miles from Ogden. The ride from Ogden to Salt Lake City is one of peculiar interest, passing down the Utah or Salt Lake Valley, sloping gently from the mountains on the one side to the Great Salt Lake on the other. In fact the railway skirts the shores of the lake for almost the entire distance. Nine miles from Ogden is Syracuse Junction, from which point the Ogden & Syracuse Railway runs to Syracuse Beach, a fine summer resort on Salt Lake. Just before entering Salt Lake City are Beck's Hot Springs, three miles out, where there are good hotel accommodations and fine baths. The medicinal qualities of the water are good, and the place is largely frequented at all seasons of the year. It is well located, and is only a few rods from the railway station.

Salt Lake City was founded July 24, 1847, by the Mormons or Latter Day Saints. The city has a population of about 35,000 people, and the elevation is 4,350 feet above sea-level. Her buildings are fine, both business blocks and private residences, and every indication of wealth is apparent. The points of interest are Fort Douglas, The Great Temple, The Tabernacle, The Assembly Hall, The Endowment House, and Zion's Co-operative Mercantile Institute. The warm sulphur baths and springs are one and a half miles north of the city, and are reached by the street-car lines.

Salt Lake City is one of the largest military posts in the West. The place attracts thousands of visitors annually, and the wide streets, lined with shade and fruit trees, bordered on either curb by clear running streams, are of themselves sights worth the long journey from the East. The luscious fruits of orchards and vineyards and the delightful view of the Wasatch Range are additional attractions. The Tabernacle is oblong, oval, and many doored. Its seating capacity is about 12,000. The roof, with one exception, is the largest self-supported roof in the world. The Great Temple, just beside it, possesses more of beauty, but it is less quaint in style. It is slowly approaching completion. Its stately walls, of polished Utah granite, rise 100 feet above the foundation, and the towers are to reach 100 feet higher. The building will be one of the most massive, imposing, and expensive churches in the world when completed. The grave of Brigham Young, his old residence, and the palace of his favorite wife, will be pointed out as objects of local interest. But from a geological standpoint the whole region merits attention. Driving to the high plateau which overlooks the city, on every hand is seen the valley, smooth, verdant, and dotted with farms. In the middle, the city peers through its myriads of leaves. Its long roads stretch into the country straight as an arrow for some fifteen miles, while to the south is seen Fort Douglas, perched upon a high knoll overlooking the city. On the inclosing hills the old water line of Great Salt Lake is visible, showing that at some time its salt waves dashed high above the dome of the Temple, and that this great valley was once an inland sea. Beneath this water-mark is another one, proving that the lake had at least two periods of sinking. The chief resort, however, is the Great Salt Lake, eighteen miles distant. This "Dead Sea of America," with its River Jordan and the distant Mount Nebo, have an interest kindred to the places of the same name in the Holy Land. The Mormons, who are inseparably identified with Salt Lake City, are a peculiar people, and, modeling their form of church government and many of their rites and ceremonies after those of the Hebrews, they have clothed the valley with a mantle of nomenclature which constantly reminds the traveler of the land from which sprang the Christian religion ; and Salt Lake City itself, with its immense Tabernacle and Great Temple, has been considered the Jerusalem of the Latter Day Saints. The fame of this city and its Mormon institutions has gone abroad into the four quarters of the globe, but its wonderful attractions for the tourist and the health and pleasure seeker, with its unlimited resources, are destined to give it a wider and more enduring fame in the near future.

Salt Lake City, at the foot of the Wasatch Mountains, and in sight of lonely Nebo, the loftiest peak of Utah, would be 28,000 feet above Nebo now if its site could take the altitude it occupied ages ago. That before becoming the bed of this lake, this site was a plateau 40,000 feet high, is clearly told in the story of the rocks. The mountains of old broke in half and settled back, leaving the valley between. The western slope of the eastern range, and the eastern slope of the western range, could some giant force bring them together, would fit almost like two cog-wheels.

CALIFORNIA POINTS.

THE YOSEMITE VALLEY.

THE Yosemite Valley is readily reached from San Francisco or **Lathrop**, via Berenda or Milton Stations, on the Los Angeles line of the Southern Pacific Railroad. Berenda is on the main line of the Southern Pacific Railroad, 178 miles from San Francisco, while Milton is on the Stockton & Copperopolis branch, which leaves the main line at Stockton, 103 miles from San Francisco. From Stockton to Milton the distance is thirty miles. From Berenda the San Joaquin Valley division of the Southern Pacific Railroad runs to Raymond, twenty-one miles distant, where there is a large and commodious hotel, and from Raymond via stage to the park. From Berenda or Milton, there are regular stages into the valley. The more preferable of the two, however, is the one from Berenda, although tourists frequently make the trip through from Berenda to Milton, visiting en route both the Mariposa and Calaveras Big Tree Groves. The round trip from San Francisco or Lathrop to the Yosemite Valley and return to San Francisco can be made in four days. This includes a visit to the Mariposa grove of big trees, either going or returning, and enables the traveler to visit all the chief points of interest in the valley. The Yosemite Valley is the tourists' paradise of California and the Pacific coast, if not of the world. It cannot be compared with Yellowstone National Park, because there are few points of similarity, and each is peerless in its own way. No other scene or series of scenes in the world presents the beauty of the one, or the wonderful features of the other. Having seen the one, the tourist should see the other. The Yosemite Valley is set apart as a park, and is dedicated to the sightseers of the world. The points of interest are El Capitan, Three Brothers, Washington Column, Cathedral Rocks, The Sentinel and Domes, Bridal Veil Falls, Yosemite Falls, Mirror Lake, and Cloud's Rest. The Yosemite Falls are composed of three cascades, the first being 1,500 feet, the second 600 feet, and the last 400 feet high. In the four days' trip from San Francisco or Lathrop, only two days can be had in the valley, which is only time enough to merely glance at the scenes of interest. A week or ten days should be spent. No pen, however graphic, can convey a correct idea of the lovely scenes which here enchant the eye.

THE MARIPOSA AND CALAVERAS BIG TREES.

The big trees which are visited en route to the Yosemite are well worth a visit. How they can be best reached is explained in the description of the Yosemite Valley. These trees are a marvelous sight. In the Mariposa group are 600 trees, of which 125 are over forty feet in circumference, and several are from ninety to one hundred feet. The Grizzly Giant, one of the monsters of this monster forest, sends out a limb which is six feet in diameter, at a height of ninety feet above the ground. The Calaveras group has one tree which is 435 feet high, and 110 feet in circumference at the butt. The Calaveras trees are most accessible from Milton, the terminus of the Stockton & Copperopolis branch of the Southern Pacific Railroad, which runs from Stockton on the Los Angeles line to Milton, just North of Lathrop. From Milton, this group of trees is forty-seven miles distant. There are also some very large trees on King's River, forty-one miles from Visalia, which is reached via the Los Angeles line of the Southern Pacific Railroad, and the Visalia Branch from Goshen. Goshen is 241 miles from San Francisco, and Visalia is fifteen miles distant from Goshen.

LOS ANGELES, SANTA BARBARA,

and San Diego, Riverside, Santa Ana, and other cities and villages in Southern California are growing in favor with tourists, invalids, and travelers generally. They are beautiful in themselves and charming in surroundings. Embowered in vines, embellished with rare flowers and fringed with orchards producing delicious fruits, they present a most enchanting and restful sight. For a winter vacation visit, Southern California is unequaled in attractions. The climate, productions, and natural scenery combine to restore health to the invalid and give enjoyment to all. In the summer the trip is also pleasant, and should not be omitted from a tour of the Golden State.

SAN FRANCISCO.

San Francisco is the pleasure seeker's great city. Its mammoth hotels, palatial in appointments as well as spacious in dimensions, can accommodate thousands. No other city on the continent has such complete and ample hotels. Adjacent and easily and quickly reached are numerous places of interest to all travelers. A score of one-day trips can be made which bring the tourist to his

San Francisco hotel every evening, and other longer journeys can be taken. The people of the city are hospitable, and have that generous disregard of expense which is so characteristic of California, and which lavishes money without stint upon public and private buildings, and in the adornment of grounds and surroundings. Every nation and every climate are represented in this most cosmopolitan of American cities, in the persons of her inhabitants and the products offered for sale in booths and buildings on her busy streets.

San Francisco is and should be made the centre from which to visit all the tourist resorts of California. It is an interesting city of itself, and will employ the time of the visitor profitably and agreeably for days. Its sail-flecked bay and the Golden Gate are a chapter of pleasing sights varied in aspect by the movements of the multitude of vessels floating the flags of all nations.

Among its many attractions the tourist must not neglect visiting the famous Cliff House, which commands a view of the Seal Rocks and the Golden Gate. The drive out to the Cliff House through the military post of Presidio and back through the park is one of the finest drives in the world. Excursions across its shining surface to the ocean, to San Rafael, etc., are enjoyable and frequent. From San Rafael the journey may be continued northward to Santa Rosa, Tomales, the Geysers, Cloverdale, and Clear Lake, passing on the return the Petrified Forest, Calistoga, St. Helena, Napa, and Vallejo. Oakland, the suburban city, in which reside many of the richest citizens of San Francisco, Mount Diablo, the Sacramento River, Sacramento, Marysville, and Mount Shasta, may all be visited at slight expense. Numerous—once famous—gold camps abound, and the stories of their rise to importance and decline to deserts form many an interesting chapter in the tales of travelers to the Pacific coast. Southward lie Santa Clara, Pescadero, San Jose, Gilroy Springs, Pajaro, Santa Cruz, and Monterey, each charming in its own way.

MONTEREY.

Frequent trains and cheap fares have built up half a score of pleasure resorts south of San Francisco, but Monterey is conceded to be the most delightful. This little city overlooks the bay of the same name, and the natural beauty of its surroundings has been heightened by the expenditure of large sums of money in hotels, parks, drives, and baths. The Hotel Del Monte, at Monterey, is the finest tourists' hotel on the Pacific coast. Excursion tickets to Monterey and return are sold in San Francisco, and as the seaside hotel is but a few hours' ride from the city it is largely patronized.

LAKE TAHOE.

Associated closely with these distinctively Californian resorts is Lake Tahoe, which lies on the boundary between California and Nevada, half in each State.

It is fourteen miles west of Carson City, the capital of Nevada, and about the same distance from Truckee, California, on the Central Pacific Railroad. This beautiful mountain lake is thirty-five miles long, fifteen miles wide, and 1,500 feet deep. Its water is as clear as crystal and as cold as ice, and though standing at an elevation of 6,700 feet above sea-level, and surrounded by mountains whose summits are white with snow nearly the whole year, it never freezes. A very pleasant side excursion trip for overland passengers can be made by leaving the Central Pacific Railroad at Reno, proceeding via Virginia & Truckee Railroad to Carson City, thence by stage to Lake Tahoe, across its surface by steamer, and return to the Central Pacific by stage, at Truckee. On the same trip Bonanza mines at Virginia City may be visited. This excursion is short and requires but little time. The lake can also be visited from Truckee, and passengers in haste to reach their destination need lose but one day.

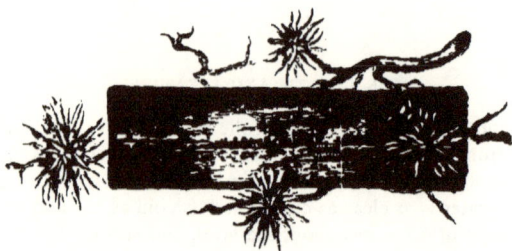

HEALTH.

I T is easy to write an apostrophe to health, for every one knows that its
value is above rubies. Yet almost wantonly, sometimes, it is sacrificed.
Nature, however, has kindly decreed that rest shall restore it, and has so
endowed a favored portion of her realm, that weary mortals may gather there, and
have brought back to them in a measure the prize they cast away. The entire
Rocky Mountain region is a sanitarium. It has the sun, the mountain breeze,
the crisp, mild air, which combine to invigorate and heal. There is no magic
in the springs, bursting and bubbling in the cañons, though the ignorant, noting
their cures, might well ascribe to them a magical power. There is no magic in
the healing wrought by a mountain summer, yet it recalls the day when the
weak were made strong by the laying on of hands. Simply marvelous are the
transformations wrought by it. Its fame has gone abroad. And winter now is
becoming entitled to a part of the honors. The West will soon be known as
an all-the-year-round resort. It deserves to be thus known. The haze of
Indian summer lingers long into the autumn, and the balminess of early autumn
gives way reluctantly for the moderate rigor of the holidays.

The invalid reaches a point, especially if his trouble is pulmonary, where a
trip, such as is suggested above, means a new lease of life to him. If he
pauses, it will soon be too late. Past a certain stage, the higher altitude of the
mountains will hasten a fatal termination, as surely as before that point is
reached it will avert it. In reading preceding chapters, the thought will occur
very properly that the outdoor life hinted at therein would be most conducive
to sound health. Such is the case. All conditions are favorable to such a life.
The beauties of Nature prompt it, and the climatic features make it agreeably
possible.

People are often puzzled to know why they are cured. What matters it so
that they are cured ? Still some analysis may be interesting. The air of Denver,
for instance, is exceedingly dry. Rain is rare. This air prevents matter which

would ordinarily become putrid, from decaying, It acts in the same manner upon diseased lungs. More than this, a greater number of cubic inches must be taken in at every breath, resulting in an expansion of the chest. It also quickens circulation wonderfully, and is about the only stimulant that gives no baneful reaction.

"The empire of climate," says Montesquieu, "is the most powerful of all empires." This airy empire has been the subject of many learned dissertations, not one of which is so convincing as the roses returning to the wannest cheek, or the dragging step once more light and buoyant. Probably the work of Chas. Denison, M. D., issued in 1880, is the most authentic ever published on the relations of climate and disease. Searching for the ideal clime, for the prevention and cure of consumption, he selects the Rocky Mountain region. He gives his reasons for this, and defends them from the stronghold of science and experience. He cites the humid, low resorts of Florida and the Carolinas and Texas, and shows that in none of their advantages can they compete with their high and dry rivals. If possessing any advantages, they are enervating, and more apt to bring the entire system down than to build it up. Of absolute cures, there are none to place to their credit. There are many credited to the greater altitudes. The book referred to is full of tabular illustrations of the points it makes.

HUNTING.

I N writing of several places, there has been incidental mention of game, but the subject deserves more specific notice. There is no excitement so thrilling and healthful as that born of the chase, and when the tremor of expectation has marred the aim, and its object flies over the hills exultant, it is genuine disappointment which follows. Hunting has been reduced to a science; but the amatuer's first idea is to find his game, and, having found it, to blaze away for general results. Until some skill has been acquired by practice the results are apt to be extremely general, but never from lack of opportunity.

Antelopes are tempting, albeit their human-like eyes beg with mute eloquence from their liquid depths for life. To find them, be up early, and gun in hand, before the sun has risen; for two hours, then, will give more shots than all the remainder of the day, for it is then they are feeding, unconscious of danger. On the vast plains, where there is often no shrub, and where the level is like a floor, it would seem that their hiding was impossible; but there are many ravines in which they may be sheltered secure from any enemy. These same ravines permit the enemy to approach under cover. Antelope meat is sweet and tender, and really creates an appetite as it crisps over the camp fire, and sends its aroma to the outer edge of the circle of light. The flesh of the mountain sheep is regarded as superior to any other trophy of the hunt, not excepting that of elk and black-tailed deer, which, before the rare toothsomeness of a juicy saddle, or the dripping ribs of a young and tender mountain sheep, is found below par. The sheep may be chased into the wildest abyss, and to the loftiest mountain tops, these difficulties only tending to make the pursuit more attractive, and many to follow it would give up buffalo, antelope, elk, and deer. North Park is surrounded by such a formation as makes it a favorite place for this game. The immense horns and the bony forehead nature has given the animal often enables it to baffle the pursuer by hurling itself from giddy heights and alighting on the protecting frontal. Or it leaps frightful chasms where no foot can follow, and if killed by an accurate bullet would only decompose far out of reach.

Buffalo are now largely confined to the plains of Wyoming and Montana, far to the North; but herds come down to within sixty miles of Cheyenne in winter. A hunter properly secreted can nearly annihilate a small herd, as the huge beasts only look around wonderingly when the one next to them is smitten to the death. The only legitimate way to hunt them is from horseback, and how fascinating it is then all border legends tell. There is some danger in it; but to the hunter that danger is but an added charm. The most formidable antagonist to be met with is the grizzly bear, which inhabits the higher ranges of the Rocky Mountains. To meet it requires a steady hand and a stout heart. The best nerve and the best weapons are not invincible. Never fire at a grizzly unless a partner is near with rifle ready poised. To come within the embrace of its mighty paws, which with one blow can break the back of an ox, is to be crushed. And yet there is nothing to which a Nimrod will point with more pride than to a grizzly's robe, with a hole through the portion which had covered the heart. This bear may be found in autumn, among the raspberry patches; but the finder will usually steal quietly away. Ten to one he has not " lost a bear." The cinnamon and common black variety attain great size, but they are lambs compared with their great cousin.

The western watercourses are most prolific of black-tailed deer, who come in little bands to drink just before sunrise or just after sunset. They are at home in an altitude which no other variety can endure, and graze in the highest parks near the summits. Generally, four or five are together. The hunter is lucky who bags more than one. It is lower down the mountain that the whistle of the elk is heard as he plunges through the forest, with his great horns laid back. It is a delightful sound to the sportsman, who steals up for a shot in the gray of the dawn. He must keep well hidden, for the eye of the elk is keen; and to the windward, for the scent is most acute. But by enough precaution a splendid shot is obtained and some magnificent bull bounds away in an instant, and falls with a crash—strong to the last. It is then that the sportsman exults.

The time was, and not many years ago, that to enjoy this sport, long excursions were necessary by horse or wagon, but now the most perfect hunting and fishing grounds are reached by the divisions of the Union Pacific Railway.

Antelope are found on all the plains adjacent to the Union Pacific Railway where there is any pasture. They abound in the parks of Colorado and Wyoming, and on the plains just east of the mountains. Jack rabbits and smaller game are met with in great numbers in the smoother portions of the mountains and on the prairies. Grizzly bear inhabit the more elevated peaks of the mountains, and are especially numerous in the Uintah and Wasatch Ranges of Utah, Wyoming, and Montana. In Colorado and Idaho they lurk about the rougher defiles, near the timber line. Black and cinnamon bear, elk, black-tailed deer, mountain sheep, and mountain lions are common to all the higher regions of the range. In Montana and Wyoming occasionally mountain goats and buffalo are brought down. Ducks, geese, brant, and other waterfowls can be found on the shores of all the rivers and lakes in the regions traversed by the Union Pacific. Nearly all the mountain brooks and lakes abound in trout and other varieties of fish. The Snake River and other tributaries of the Columbia are filled with salmon. The angler can scarcely go amiss in any part of the region above named. Prairie chicken, sage-hen, quail, snipe, and other land birds are abundant everywhere. Eagles are picked off the peaks of the Rockies occasionally. In short, the country tributary to the Union Pacific Railway everywhere presents attractions to the sportsman. Perhaps the most famous and favorite hunting-ground of North America to-day, is that portion of Wyoming lying north of Rock Creek and Rawlins. In that region can be found all varieties of game, from the mountain squirrel to the grizzly bear, and from the harmless beaver to the bellowing buffalo. Transportation thither can be engaged at Cheyenne, Laramie, Rock Creek, or Rawlins. Arrangements should be made for camping out, and from two to six weeks should be spent in the field to thoroughly enjoy the sport. The North Park of Colorado is another famous hunting ground where the largest game abounds. Two hunters in one season brought fourteen large wagon-loads to market. They killed 500 antelope and 250 elk. Herds of 500 elk are frequently seen. The Bear River country, in Idaho, Utah, and Wyoming has been a glorious region for disciples of the gun and rod since the earliest days of its discovery. But, as said before, the hunter or fisherman can find rare sport in almost any portion of the territory tributary to the Union Pacific Railway.

FISHING.

MENTION has been made in these pages of fishing, but the following additional matter will prove of interest to the lovers of the "gentle science."

Among the several varieties of food-fish which are found in the streams of Colorado, Wyoming, Idaho, Montana, Utah, Oregon, and Washington, may be mentioned speckled mountain brook trout, silver trout, black trout, common trout, bass, pike, pickerel, salmon, etc., some twenty-five or more species abounding in the western watercourses. Particular attention is called to the speckled mountain brook trout, here so common, for it is considered the finest food-fish, as well as the "gamiest" of all the finny tribe, and consequently affords more sport to the angler.

Fly fishing for trout is good during the months of July, August, September, and October. Bait fishing is generally good during the early summer. The angle worm is good bait the world over. Besides the artificial bait, which can be procured anywhere, nature provides an abundance of flies and worms along every stream, which the angler can readily find.

Good trout fields are found in Platte Cañon, South Park, Middle Park, North Park, and Estes Park ; in Clear Creek Cañon, Green Lake, near George-town, and in Boulder Cañon, all in Colorado ; in Blackfoot Creek, near Soda Springs, Idaho ; in Yellowstone National Park, and in almost all the mountain streams of Montana, Utah, Oregon, and Washington, particularly in the northern streams of Idaho, around Hailey, Ketchum, and Boise City.

The trout, from its extreme beauty, delicacy of flavor, and extraordinary activity as a game fish, has attracted the attention of all classes of people, from the boy with a pin hook, to those who have swayed the destiny of empire. The divine, the philosopher, the poet, the artist, and the statesman, from the earliest dates, have enjoyed many days of recreation in his pursuit, sang songs to his praise, or written pages of instruction of their own experience in taking him from his native element.

There are three different methods pursued in the capture of the trout : angling at the top, with a natural or artificial fly, grasshopper, or other small insect ; at the middle, with a minnow, shrimp, or similar small fish ; and at the bottom, with a worm, or different kinds of pastes.

Fly Fishing.—Fly fishing is usually practiced with a short, one-handed rod, from ten to twelve feet in length, or a two-handed rod from fifteen to eighteen feet in length. The first mentioned is the most common in use, and is calculated for the majority of mountain streams, which are small and require but little length of rod or line.   Attached to the rod should be a reel, containing from thirty to fifty yards of hair, grass, silk, or silk and hair line; the latter description should be used if it can be procured, tapering from the tenth of an inch almost to a point; to this should be attached a leader of from one to two yards in length; and finally the fly, on a light length of gut; if two or three flies are used, place them on the leader with short gut, about twenty-four inches apart.

The latter description of rod is used in larger streams, where it is necessary to throw a great distance; for this purpose, the reel should be large enough to contain 100 yards of line, with the other tackle precisely the same as with the smaller rod.   It should be recollected that the trout rods should be made similar to the salmon rods, and of the lightest woods.

MINNOW FISHING.—The rod used in this kind of angling is from twelve to sixteen feet in length, with a stiffer top than that used for fly fishing, and goes under the name of a bait-rod.   The smaller, say twelve feet, for small wading streams, and the longer for wider and deeper waters.   Attached should be an American reel, holding from thirty to fifty yards of American laid grass, or silk line, with from two to three yards of silk-worm gut, terminating with a Limerick hook, from number two to five, according to the size of the bait, fastened by a loop as before described.   For baiting the minnow, pass the hook in at the mouth and out at the gills, then in again at the commencement of the dorsal fin and out again just beyond, tying the hook at each end with a piece of thin silk or thread.   By this method, a live minnow can be kept animated for a great length of time.

WORM FISHING.—This is, and has been, from the earliest periods, the standard mode of trout angling.   It is practiced principally at the opening and closing of the season by anglers generally.   The rod generally used is from twelve to fifteen feet in length for small streams, and from fifteen to twenty feet (according to circumstances) for the larger.   The reel, and other appurtenances, should be similar to that described for minnow fishing.

The various fish commissioners who have supervision of the public waters, and the collection, propagation, culture, and distribution of fish, have done much to increase the numbers, varieties, and improve the quality of fish in the western waters.

SOME OF THE POINTS OF INTEREST WHICH ARE MENTIONED IN THE PRECEDING PAGES.

ELEVATIONS OF PRINCIPAL MOUNTAIN CITIES, PEAKS, AND PASSES.

COLORADO.

CITIES AND TOWNS.	ELEVATION.	PEAKS.	ELEVATION.	PASSES.	ELEVATION.
Alpine	9,175	Antero	14,245	Alpine	12,124
Alpine Tunnel	11,623	Arapahoe	13,520	Argentine	13,100
Black Hawk	8,057	Audubon	13,173	Berthoud	11,349
Boreas	11,498	Bald	11,493	Boulder	11,670
Boulder	5,331	*Blanca	14,464	Breckenridge	11,560
Breckenridge	9,555	Byers	12,778	Cochetopa	10,032
Buena Vista	7,957	Ethel	11,976	Cunningham	12,090
Central City	8,510	Evans	14,321	Fremont	11,325
Denver	5,203	Gray's	14,441	Georgia	11,811
Dillon	8,840	Hahn's	10,906	Gove	9,590
Dome Rock	6,227	Harvard	14,375	Hamilton	12,370
Estabrook Park	7,578	Holy Cross	14,176	Hayden	10,780
Fort Collins	4,976	Irwin's	14,336	Hoosier	11,500
Georgetown	8,560	James	13,283	Lake Fork	12,540
Golden	5,710	Long's	14,271	Loveland	11,500
Greeley	4,670	Massive	14,298	Marshall	10,852
Gunnison	7,582	Monitor	11,270	Poncho	8,945
Heywood Springs	8,093	Princeton	14,196	Raton	7,863
Idaho Springs	7,567	Pike's	14,147	Tarryall	12,176
Keystone	9,149	Rosalie	14,340	Trout Creek	9,346
Leadville	10,209	Vale	14,187	Tennessee	10,700
		Uncompahgre	14,419	Veta	9,339

WYOMING.

CITIES AND TOWNS.	ELEVATION.	PEAKS.	ELEVATION.	PEAKS.	ELEVATION.
Cheyenne	6,038	Fremont's	13,750	Cloud	13,000
Sherman	8,235	Laramie	10,000	Grand Encampment	11,053
Laramie	7,137	Gilbert's	13,250	Pelham	11,524
Evanston	6,747	Snow's	13,570		

UTAH AND IDAHO.

CITIES AND TOWNS.	ELEVATION.	PEAKS.	ELEVATION.	CITIES AND TOWNS.	ELEVATION.
Salt Lake City	4,350	Martineau, U. T.	7,800	Soda Springs, I. T.	5,779
Ogden, Utah	4,294	Nebo, U. T.	12,000	Sawtooth, I. T.	7,000
Logan, Utah	4,504	Blackfoot, I. T.	7,490	Oxford, I. T.	4,862
Blackfoot, I. T.	4,512	Custer, I. T.	8,760	Silver City, I. T.	6,680
Boise City, I. T.	2,800	Estes, I. T.	10,050	Idaho City, I. T.	4,623
Bonanza City, I. T.	6,400	Grand Teton, I. T.	13,691	Lewiston, I. T.	680
Galena, I. T.	7,900	Soda, I. T.	9,683		

MONTANA.

CITIES AND TOWNS.	ELEVATION.	PEAKS.	ELEVATION.	PASSES.	ELEVATION.
Helena	4,266	Bridger's	9,002	Deer Lodge	5,808
Butte	5,492	Emigrant	10,629	Flathead	6,769
Deer Lodge	4,532	Electric	10,992	Bridger	6,147
Virginia City	2,824	Liberty	9,162	Lewis and Clarke	6,323
Missoula	3,900	Blackmore	10,134	Little Blackfoot	6,250
Argenta	6,337	Delano	10,200	Mullen	5,980
Bozeman	4,900	Sphinx	10,880	Madison	6,911

PRINCIPAL PEAKS OF THE SIERRA NEVADA AND COAST RANGES.

PEAKS.	ELEVATION.	PEAKS.	ELEVATION.	PEAKS.	ELEVATION.
Globe Peak, Nev.	11,237	Mt. Olympus, W. T.	8,138	†Mount Whitney, Cal.	15,088
Mt. Hood, Ore.	14,000	Mt. Baker, W. T.	11,100	Mt. Tyndall, Cal.	14,386
Mt. Pitt, Ore.	11,000	Mt. San Bernardino, Cal.	11,600	Mt. Williams, Cal.	14,500
Mt. St. Helens, W. T.	9,750	Mt. Shasta, Cal.	14,444	Mt. Kaweah, Cal.	14,000
Mt. Adams, W. T.	9,570	Mt. Diablo, Cal.	3,856	Mt. Gardner, Cal.	14,000
Mt. Ranier, W. T.	12,360	Mt. Tamalpais, Cal.	2,604	Mt. Brown, Cal.	13,886
Mt. Constance, W. T.	7,777	Mt. St. Helena, Cal.	4,343		

* Highest Peak in Colorado.   † Highest Peak in the United States.